J
789.99
K   Kettelkamp, Larry.
            Electronic musical instruments : what
        they do, how they work / Larry Kettel-
        kamp ; foreword by Herbert Deutsch. —
        New York : W. Morrow, 1984.

            122 p. : ill.   wc 5-9
            SUMMARY: Explains the principles of
        electronic music, discusses the uses of
        such electronic instruments as oscilla-
        tors, synthesizers, electronic organs.
            ISBN 0-688-02781-4 : 9.00
            1. Musical instruments, Electronic. 2. Elec-
        tronic music.

electronic musical instruments

electronic musical instruments

What They Do, How They Work

LARRY KETTELKAMP

Foreword by Herbert Deutsch

WILLIAM MORROW AND COMPANY
New York · 1984

PHOTO CREDITS: Permission for the following photographs is gratefully acknowl-edged: Allen Organ Company, pp. 58, 59 both; Brian Ballweg, p. 35; Barcus-Berry, pp. 16 both, 18 all; Casio Inc., pp. 77, 97; Gibson, Division of Norlin Industries, Inc., pp. 88, 91; Hohner Inc., pp. 23-25; Jonathan Sa'adah, p. 80 all; Korg Keyboard Photos, Courtesy of Unicord, Westbury, N.Y., pp. 41, 50 top; Lowrey, pp. 62 both, 64 both; Moog Music Inc., pp. 36, 39, 42 both, 49, 50 bottom; MXR Innovations Inc., pp. 67, 69 top; Rodgers Organ Company, p. 56; Roland Corp. U.S., pp. 47, 52 both, 53 both, 69 bottom, 70, 73, 82, 93, 94, 107; Rhodes Keyboard Instruments, pp. 21 both, 22 both; Yamaha International Corp., pp. 13 both, 14, 101 top, 113.

Library of Congress Cataloging in Publication Data
Kettelkamp, Larry.   Electronic musical instruments.
Includes index. Summary: Explains the principles of electronic music, discusses the uses of such electronic instruments as oscillators, synthesizers, electronic organs, and sound processors, and gives advice on performing and recording electronic mu-sic. 1. Musical instruments, Electronic. [1. Musical instruments, Electronic. 2. Elec-tronic music] I. Title.   ML1092.K47   1984   789.9'9   83-23819
ISBN 0-688-02781-4 (reinforced trade ed.)

CONTENTS

FOREWORD

In September 1965, I was putting together a concert with a group called The New York Improvisation Quartet. During the final preparations, my young daughter was with me at the office of the concert promoter. His associate struck up a conversation with my little girl. "What instrument does your daddy play?" he asked. With straight-ahead, four-year-old honesty, she replied, "The tape recorder."

We already had entered the Age of Electronic Musical Instruments in the sixties, and a good bit of electronic music had begun to emerge. Bob Moog had recently sold his first synthesizers, Donald Buchla had designed *his* instrument, and the Columbia-Princeton Electronic Music Studio was in high gear. There were even a few advanced-thinking individuals who were learning to create music on computers.

Most people were completely unaware of these developments, however. Rock music was in its early stages and hadn't moved from a guitar-based style. Most groups didn't have keyboard players yet, and amplifiers were used for loudness, not for effects. TV commercials and films were still orchestrated with traditional acoustic instruments, but things were beginning to change . . . *and change they did* . . . as the new and exciting electronic musical instruments began to catch on. Now, within a few short years, we have reached a stage where music and electronics are comfortably interrelated. Microcomputer developments have led to the design of surprisingly sophisticated instruments. Some are so inexpensive that they are sold in drugstores and department stores as "impulse" items.

When Larry Kettelkamp first discussed his concept of this book with me, I was delighted with the idea. He already had written four other books on the "families" of musical instruments, and he viewed this new group of electronic musical instruments as a logical extension of musical growth in a technological world, and the newest instrumental family. In a sense, that is precisely what it is. Electronic instruments, whether they are synthesizers, electronic organs, electronic pianos, electric guitars, computers (and, oh yes, even tape recorders!), have joined the world of music as we know it today.

Now interested students can learn about the synthesis of electronic music right along with their study of music theory, harmony, and the other musical rudiments. Hundreds of colleges and universities have extensive studios for electronic and computer music studies. Synthesizer, electric piano, and electric guitar labs are found in high schools and junior high schools. Everywhere you turn, electronic musical instruments can be heard. From new wave and disco to the corner arcade and the home computer, you hear what has become the sound of today.

When my daughter first talked about her daddy as a musician who played the tape recorder, there was still a considerable amount of mystery surrounding the electronic music world. Now, with the field such a large one, the unknown can no longer exist. By providing a short history of these instruments, an introduction to the ways in which they operate and a look at some of the specific instruments available, Larry Kettelkamp takes away those mysteries and provides a very nice starting point for exploration into this field. Those who are interested in exploring electronic music with an eye toward a future profession will find this book a valuable reference. Those who have a curiosity about why and how things are the way they are will find it a fascinating look at another facet of the way man celebrates himself through music.

Herbert Deutsch
Professor of Music; Director, Electronic Music Studio
Hofstra University, Hempstead, N.Y.
Assistant to the President
Moog Music Inc., Buffalo, N.Y.

INTRODUCTION

Today there is a revolution in music. Over the last few decades musical instruments have become both electric and electronic. Ordinary instruments such as flutes, saxophones, clarinets, and trumpets are played into microphones so that their sounds can then be amplified, modified, and controlled. Going a step further, these woodwind and brass instruments, together with guitars, basses, pianos, and even drums, now also use ingenious "pickup" microphones attached directly to the instruments or even permanently built in. Many new instruments, including synthesizers, electronic pianos, and pipeless organs, now produce purely electronic sound. Of this vast array of electric and electronic instruments, some still closely resemble their natural cousins, while others have both new shapes and functions.

Along with the new instruments have come many clever devices that can alter and process sounds electronically, making them bright or strident, dull or muffled, fuzzy, strange, pulsing, echoing, or multiplied in unusual ways. And with the advances in computer technology, sounds can easily be created, duplicated, and stored—that is, remembered by digital computers that are built into the new instruments. Sounds never heard before can be constructed, or electronically synthesized instantly, and such sounds already are becoming a part of everyday music in the home, in performing groups, and in both serious and pop recordings.

Advancing technology brings ongoing advantages to the whole realm of electronic music. Space-age microcircuits make electronic instruments more versatile, yet smaller, simpler, more portable, and less expensive than ever before. Prices ranging from $100 to $1000 make quality instruments available to young people at home or at school. Access brings familiarity, so that the new generation of music-makers and listeners will become completely at home with electronic sound and electronic instruments.

This book introduces the new world of electric and electronic musical instruments. You will learn how instruments—from brass, woodwind, and percussion, to guitars, and vibraphones—become electric and how their sounds are amplified. You will read how electronic instruments and devices, such as synthesizers, electronic pianos, electronic organs, computer rhythm units, amplifiers, and special sound processors have developed, what they are capable of doing, and how they are used in performance and recording. You also will find suggestions for purchasing your own electronic instruments and sound processing devices, with step-by-step examples of how to use and combine them effectively.

─1─

INSTRUMENTS GO ELECTRIC

AMPLIFIED SOUNDS

A typical musical combo today is a varied mixture. You may see such instruments as guitar, piano, organ or synthesizer, drums and cymbals, trumpet, and saxophone, as well as vocalists who frequently double on some of the instruments. Whatever the mix, all of the sounds will be coming from oversized loudspeakers. This is true even though some of these instruments and also the voices of the singers are purely acoustic—that is, they produce natural sounds that do not require amplification. However, both the instruments and voices vary in natural volume as well as tone quality, or color.

For example, without amplification an acoustic guitar would sound faint at the back of a large room. And the penetrating sounds of a trumpet combined with other instruments would tend to drown out the vocalist's voice.

The solution to balancing these sounds is to place microphones in front of the acoustic instruments. Frequently they are on stands with boom extensions that allow the mikes to reach to any desired location. For picking up a guitar a mike can be pointed at the open soundhole from a distance of a few inches. With a flute it can be placed next to the mouthpiece. Or with a trumpet, already a loud instrument, the microphone can be several feet in front of the bell.

The microphones are connected to mixing and amplifying devices, and the sounds are reproduced through loudspeakers. Once the sounds are captured by the mikes, their qualities now depend on the electronic devices. They are not only made louder, but through tone settings and other controls they can be changed in many ways. The sounds of a guitar and vocalist, for instance, can be made brighter so they are heard as clearly as the wind instruments and percussion. Or a piano can be brought "forward" for a solo or dropped into the background for accompaniment. The entire level and quality can be adjusted to the performing room, no matter how large it may be. The natural sounds are beginning to "go electric."

ELECTRIC PICKUPS

Any device that converts one type of energy into another is called a *transducer*. An ordinary microphone on a stand is one type of transducer used to convert sound energy to electrical energy.

Another type is what is commonly called a *pickup*. This is simply a small microphone that converts vibrations directly from part of the instrument itself. The simplest sound pickup is a contact microphone. This can be placed against the vibrating surface of any ordinary musical instrument. It is held in place with sticky mastic, which keeps it firmly in contact with the vibrating material.

String instruments such as the guitar, violin, and piano all produce their sounds by means of strings set into vibration. The strings are stretched across a bridge that is firmly in contact with the sounding board to pass along the vibrations of the stretched strings. The electrically amplified sound from such an instrument is usually most natural when the contact microphone is either attached directly to the bridge or to the sounding board very near the bridge, where vibrations are strongest.

For the violin family of instruments a tiny contact mike may be clamped to one edge of the vertical bridge beneath the strings. For a piano a pair of contact microphones may give the best results. For example, one mike can be fastened to the sounding board while another is fastened to the frame, or *harp*. An electrical mixing unit with volume and tone controls permits the sounds of the two pickups to be blended so the total sound is neither too bright nor too dull.

To amplify an ordinary classical or folk guitar, a narrow bar-shaped microphone is clamped across the open hole directly beneath the strings. On an *f*-hole guitar a similar flat bar microphone lies against the sounding board beneath the strings. It can be positioned exactly along a guiding rod running parallel to the strings.

Since a guitar pickup microphone is very close to the strings, the amplified sound is mostly that of the strings alone. The sounding board and hollow soundbox of the guitar are no longer needed to reinforce the sounds. So on the modern electric guitar the sound box can be replaced by a solid piece of wood or plastic made in any shape desired.

For an electric guitar, a typical pickup consists of a row of small magnets, placed one beneath each string. Usually each magnet can be raised or lowered to increase or decrease the volume of its string. The closer to the string, the louder the sound. There is a tiny coil of wire surrounding but not touching each magnet. When a steel string vibrates, the magnet beneath it induces a tiny current in the surrounding coil. This current then can be made stronger by an amplifier.

The sound an electric guitar makes depends on the vibrations of a stretched string. These vibrations are complex. First the string is plucked to set it into mo-

The Yamaha SBG2000 solid body electric guitar *(left)* and the
Yamaha SA2000 combination acoustic/electric guitar *(right)*. Note
that each guitar has two rows of magnetic pickups, volume and
tone controls, and a three-way toggle switch for detecting back and
front pickups individually or blending both sounds.

tion. The entire string vibrates as a unit to create the basic, or *fundamental,* pitch of the string. At the same time the string also divides into vibrating sections. It will vibrate in two equal sections, three equal sections, four equal sections and so on. The sectional vibrations all "ride along" with the simple vibrations of the full string. The sectional vibrations, called *partials* or *overtones,* blend with the fundamental pitch. The total mixture of vibrations creates the quality, or *timbre,* of the string sound. Only one sound is heard but it has the special quality that identifies it as guitar sound.

Most electric guitars have two rows of pickup magnets. If one pickup unit is placed near the bridge, it detects mainly the partial, or *harmonic,* vibrations of the strings, yielding a thin, bright sound. If a second

A Yamaha BB2000 solid body electric bass guitar with dual magnetic pickups, separate pickup volume controls, and a three-way toggle switch.

pickup is placed further from the bridge, this detects the fundamental vibrations of the strings, yielding a mellow sound. Volume can be adjusted for each pickup, and switches permit either pickup to be heard separately, or both to be blended.

A unique electric instrument called the steel guitar is mounted on a stand. It has no sound box, and as with other electric guitars, the sound is detected by magnetic pickups. But instead of being pressed against metal frets to shorten them, the strings are shortened or lengthened by a bar, or *steel*, pressed across them with the left hand. The bar slides back and forth along the strings, making the pitches glide up and down. This "Hawaiian" effect is a natural part of the sound. If the player shifts the bar slightly back and forth regularly, the sound takes on an undulation like a pleasant singing voice. This is called *vibrato*.

The bar can cover the strings only at a few specific angles. Because this limits the choice of chords, the steel guitar is provided with some extra ways for making pitch changes. Some guitars have several foot pedals, connected to one end of a particular string. When a pedal is pushed down it stretches that string tighter to raise the pitch by one *semitone*, or one half-step, of the musical octave. The pedal can be depressed quickly, or gradually to create a gliding effect. Some steel guitars are built with two or even three separate necks, each with its own set of strings. There may be as many as eight or ten strings on each neck. The player can choose a separate tuning for any of the sets of strings. Thus, with foot pedals, extra necks, and extra strings, the player can make the many changes of chords and pitches needed for almost any music.

Electrical technology also has been applied to the

An electric violin with volume control *(left)*. A vertical vibration guitar transducer *(above)*.

violin. Some violins are now made with a *transducer,* a device that converts mechanical vibrations to electrical energy, permanently embedded in the bridge. Wires may be hidden inside the hollow body of the violin, and a volume control can be mounted on the arched top. Or as with the guitar, the soundbox can be replaced by a solid piece of wood with internal cutouts to hold electrical wires and controls. The tone then is simply that of the bowed strings, amplified and modified through tone controls.

The electric bass viol has become a popular combo instrument. It comes in two basic styles. The first looks like the acoustic string bass, but with a narrower and shallower body. It is played in upright position, with the four strings plucked in rhythm style. If needed, a bow can be used for sustained sounds. The tone is amplified directly from a pickup beneath the strings. The second style is in the form of a bass guitar with frets and an extended neck. The instrument is built like a solid-body guitar, and is plucked with the fingertips in the same manner as the upright bass. With either instrument the strings are slapped against the fingerboard for solid rhythmic accents.

With wind instruments transducers vary. For those with single vibrating reeds like clarinet and sax a narrow unit can be locked under the metal clamp that

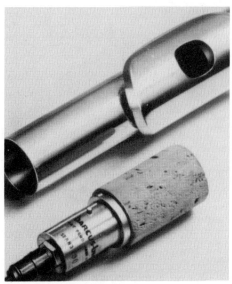

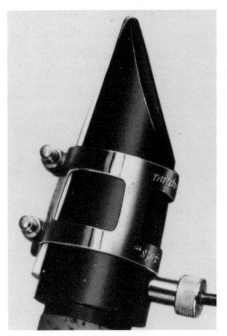

Barcus-Berry transducers for wind instruments: a flute end-cork mike transducer *(top right)*; a clarinet/saxophone mike transducer and detail of a reed transducer *(above and center)*; a brass mouthpiece mike transducer *(right)*.

holds the reed to the mouthpiece. Thus vibrations are picked up directly from the reed itself.

A higher-quality system uses a tiny microphone only one-quarter inch wide. A hole of the same diameter must be bored into the instrument tubing near the mouthpiece. The microphone inserted into the sidewall then picks up vibrations from the air column inside without disturbing the playing of the instrument. This method can be used with both the reeds and the brass instruments. Since the flute already has a removable end cork on the head joint where the sound is produced, this can easily be replaced with a cork containing the same kind of tiny microphone.

Transducers are available even for percussion instruments. These are normally of the contact type. Sticky mastic holds them firmly to the surfaces of drumheads, cymbals, or wood blocks. Each unit is attached wherever the amplified sound is most natural.

The vibraphone or vibraharp, called "vibes" for short, is a partially electric percussion instrument. It has metal tone bars graduated in size, with resonating tubes beneath them. Just inside each tube a metal disk spins on a shaft. A small electric motor rotates the shaft several times per second. The exact speed can be selected by the player, either by changing the speed of the motor or by changing a belt to a smaller or larger pulley. The rotating disks add an undulation to the sustained sounds, giving the vibraphone its haunting singing quality. Felt dampers operated by a foot pedal can stop the bars from ringing.

Among the most cleverly designed electric instruments in this broad category are the electric pianos. Designed to be highly portable, they are compact instruments. Each has a keyboard coupled to some mechanism for striking various materials, such as short, stretched strings, metal bars, or even brass reeds. The sounds are then highly amplified.

One electric piano, the Rhodes Mark II, has a series of metal rods, each looking like half of a tuning fork. The key action is like an ordinary piano's, only simplified. When a key is depressed, it throws a tiny plunger upward to strike the metal rod. As on an ordinary piano, the speed at which the key is depressed controls the volume of the sound. A sustaining pedal like that on a regular piano controls a row of felt dampers. When the pedal is pressed the dampers are released, allowing the rods to continue to vibrate. For fine tuning, a spring slides back and forth along the stem or tine of each rod. Sliding it toward the vibrating end raises the pitch while sliding it toward the base of the tine lowers the pitch.

The faint sound of each rod is detected by a magnetic pickup, converted to electrical impulses and amplified. There is an overall volume control for the piano. Bass and treble controls are available to make the sound

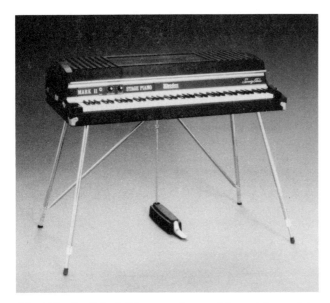

The Rhodes Mark II stage piano with sustain pedal and stand.

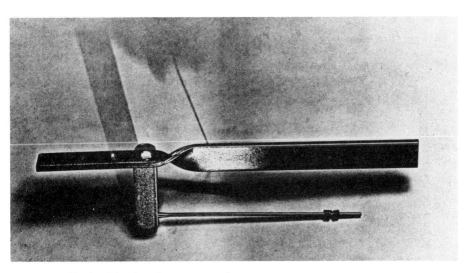

Detail of a Rhodes tine, or tone bar.

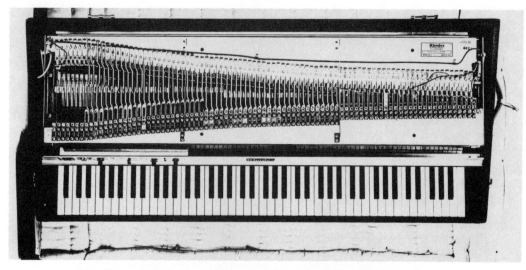

Top view of the Rhodes electric piano, showing metal "forks," or tines, of graduated size. The tines are struck from below as the keys are depressed, and their soft sounds are detected by magnetic pickups.

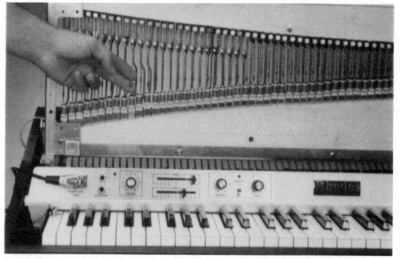

Tuning and adjusting the Rhodes electric piano.

brighter or deeper. An additional control can be used to add vibrato to the piano sound, creating a shimmering effect. Connection cords, called *patch cords,* hook up the keyboard unit to combined amplifier-speaker units.

Another kind of electric piano, called the Pianet, is built by the Hohner Company, makers of accordions and harmonicas with metal reeds. The tones of the Pianet also are produced by metal reeds. When a key is pushed down, a suction pad at the other end pulls up on the reed to which it is attached, then releases it with

The tones of the Hohner Pianet T electric piano are produced by brass reeds.

Detail of the Pianet T, showing brass reeds of graduated size. When a key is depressed, a suction cup releases the reed with a snap. The reed vibrations are detected by magnetic pickups.

a snap so the reed can vibrate freely. Movements of the tip of the reed affect a tiny electromagnet, which converts the vibrations to electrical impulses. These are then fed to a conventional amplifier.

A companion to the Pianet is the Clavinet, also designed by Hohner. This is built like the early keyboard instrument called the clavichord. Short strings run horizontally beneath the keyboard assembly. When a key is depressed, a plunger presses a string smartly against a metal edge called an anvil. The action is something like striking a piano string with a dinner knife. The string then vibrates between the anvil and one anchored end. The unused part of the string is damped with felt to prevent it from vibrating. As with a real clavichord, the sounds are faint. However, magnetic pickups convert the vibrations to electrical patterns, which can be amplified to the needed volume.

The manufacturers of the Clavinet and Pianet now also offer a combination instrument, the Clavinet-Pianet DUO, which contains both reeds and strings. Controlled with a single keyboard, the sounds of plucked reeds or strings can be voiced alone, or combined in various ways.

The Hohner Clavinet-Pianet DUO combines the sounds of brass reeds and short strings. Its faint sounds are amplified electronically.

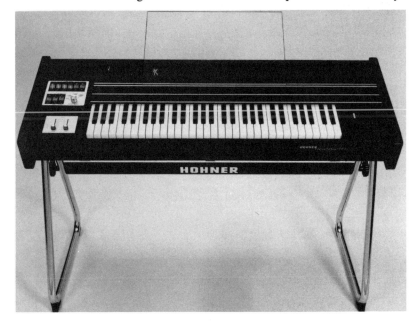

2

INSTRUMENTS GO ELECTRONIC

DEVELOPING ELECTRONIC SOUND

Electronic sound developed from the invention of vacuum tubes in the early 1900s. These tubes made it possible to take feeble electrical impulses and strengthen them, so that identical but much stronger electrical impulses were generated. This was called *amplification*. The electrical output of the tube amplifier was connected to a coil of wire surrounding a magnet inside a loudspeaker. When the stepped-up electrical impulses passed through the coil, it was set into vibration along with the speaker cone to which it was attached. These vibrations passed through the air and amplified sounds of great volume were heard.

26

Electronic amplification coincided closely with the development of both radio and the magnetic tape recorder. Studios were designed for broadcasting and recording sound, and experimentation with sound began. The basic equipment used in such studios could both alter and create sound. For example, tape-recorded sounds could be played fast or slow, backward or forward, and tapes could easily be cut apart and spliced together in all sorts of combinations. Thus, new sounds could be made out of old ones. Furthermore, special devices called electrical oscillators could create noises— buzzes, whistles, sirens, and bleeps of an amazing variety. These devices led to the beginnings of purely electronic music and to the development of electronic musical instruments.

Electronic music-making began seriously in Europe in the 1950s. In France the government provided money for a special recording and composing studio. French engineers and composers worked together. They were especially interested in using tape recordings of natural sounds, from outdoor and city street noises to the sounds of machinery, musical instruments, human speech, and singing. The tape recordings were speeded up to make the sounds higher in pitch, or slowed down to make them lower in pitch. Short sounds were made long and long sounds were cut apart to make short ones. Tapes were run backward so that the recorded sounds started and stopped in entirely different ways. Thus all of the natural recorded sounds became raw material to be altered and spliced with the tape equipment. The familiar sounds became new and strange and were combined to make new compositions and recordings.

In 1951 German engineers and composers pioneered the use of electronic oscillators, which generate purely electronic sound. A government-funded studio opened in Cologne, and composers started working enthusiastically on electronic music, using the new devices. In the same year, Columbia University in New York City purchased an Ampex tape recorder. Composers there experimented with the tape recorder to develop original music. Soon Princeton University in New Jersey joined Columbia to form the Columbia-Princeton Electronic Music Studio.

In 1959 RCA engineers designed a complete electronic music-making system for the Columbia-Princeton center in New York. Using oscillator-generated tones, it was able to create an almost endless variety of new sounds for composing music. Thus, the American studio stressed the use of both prerecorded tape sounds and purely electronically generated sounds in the development of new music, a combination that still forms the basic building blocks of most of the electronic music of today.

OSCILLATORS

The work done in any electronic device depends on the manipulation of the basic properties of electricity. Atoms have negative charges called *electrons.* Electrons can accumulate in certain places, and these negative charges will flow, or transfer, to places having fewer electrons. The force of such a transfer is called *voltage,* and the transfer of total electric charge past a certain point is called *current.*

Current can flow in a single direction, and so is called direct current, or *DC.* Or it can regularly reverse directions, and then is called alternating current, or *AC.* The rate at which it alternates is the *frequency,* and the amount, or strength, of the current is called the *amplitude.* The job of an amplifier is to manipulate and boost electrical voltage, current, and amplitude.

In order to have electronic sound one must have an electronic oscillator. This is how it works. First an electrical circuit is made to alternate, or vibrate. Some of this electrical output is fed back to the original circuit so that the vibrations are reinforced. When the energy gained through the feedback is more than the loss, the circuit becomes a self-generator, or *oscillator.*

An example of such feedback is the howl that can develop in a public address, or P.A. system, consisting of a microphone, an amplifier, and several loudspeakers. This happens when the microphone is placed too close to the loudspeakers. Then the sound coming from the loudspeakers gets back to the microphone, re-combining with the original sound going into the micro-phone. This feedback loop continues to build up inside the amplifier until it sets up its own vibration. The am-plifier has then become an oscillator.

The human ear is sensitive to sound vibrations from about 20 to 20,000 Hz. *Hz* is an abbreviation for (Heinrich) Hertz, the name of one of the pioneering scientists in the study of electricity, and stands for "cy-cles per second." Whenever an electronic oscillator generates a frequency within this range, the resulting sound is a steady squawk, squeal, or buzz, which can be made audible to the human ear. The device is then called an *audio* oscillator, meaning "sound" oscillator, and the frequency it generates is called the *audio signal.* This oscillator sound is the raw material from which synthesized music is built.

On most equipment using oscillator sounds there are control knobs, buttons, or sliders marked with geo-metric shapes. There are three common shapes. The first looks like the slanted teeth of a saw, the second like a row of triangles, and the third like a row of squares. These shapes are called *wave-forms.* A wave-form is the path, or shape, of a single, back-and-forth electrical vibration as it appears on the screen of an oscilloscope.

The three basic wave-forms—sawtooth, triangular,

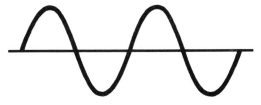

sine wave (sounds like a mellow flute)

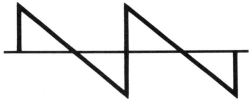

sawtooth wave (sounds like a trumpet or bowed strings)

triangular wave (sounds like a recorder)

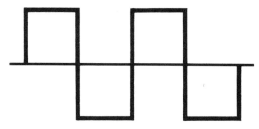

square wave (sounds like a clarinet)

random waves (sound like noise)

Common oscillator wave-forms.

and square—appear as simple shapes. However, each represents complex sound made up of a fundamental, or basic pitch frequency, and many partial vibrations or higher overtones combined. The purest sound that can be produced by any tone generator is called a *sine wave,* a mathematical curve with a smoothly rounded shape. Such a sound carries no extra overtones. Its timbre is very pure, like that of a mellow flute or whistle. Perhaps the best example is the sound of a tuning fork held near the ear. By comparison, the sound of a sawtooth wave resembles that of an oboe or trumpet. The triangular wave sounds a little like a wooden recorder. And the square wave sounds like a clarinet.

If sine waves are combined in smaller and smaller amounts in the natural harmonic series (at frequencies of two, three, four, and five times the fundamental), the result is a wave-form that gradually takes on a sawtooth shape. In the same way, the square wave and the triangular wave also are combinations of a rich blending of overtones.

The vibrations of an oscillator can also produce a jagged, irregular wave-form. In this case many random and unrelated pitch frequencies from high to low are produced all at once. Since the resulting sound cannot be recognized by any single tonal frequency, it seems pitchless. If heard in a sudden burst, it is like the sound of a percussion instrument. Heard continuously, it is like static or the constant noise of a waterfall.

Altogether the wave-forms and tones that can be generated by an electronic oscillator range through all possible colors and blends from pure music to pure noise. Such oscillator-produced sounds, along with their combinations and variations, are at the heart of all electronic music.

SYNTHESIZERS

The principle of the electronic oscillator led to the development of the completely electronic musical instrument called the *synthesizer*. Unlike all instruments that came before it, it has no stretched strings, mechanical strikers, or vibrating parts, yet it produces complete musical sounds, noises, and rhythms. Purely electronic devices are made to generate, alter, and control sound in almost unbelievable ways.

To synthesize means to build. And this is exactly what a synthesizer does. It builds sounds of every type—bright or mellow, crisp or smooth, beautiful or noisy—and as high or low as the ear can hear. The principles of sound synthesis are behind all electronic instruments, from keyboard units to electronic organs and sound processors.

One of the first complete synthesizers was the huge studio complex designed by RCA engineers for the Columbia-Princeton Electronic Music Center. Named the RCA Mark II, it was built of many separate units, called *modules,* each with a particular job to do. Some modules generated sounds, while others altered them. The modules could be interconnected in many different ways. The RCA synthesizer could electronically generate sounds of almost any kind. In addition, it could be programmed to follow certain sound-processing rules and steps automatically through the insertion of punched computer cards.

Like the RCA Mark II, the first large synthesizers all were built with separate modules that could be wired, or "patched," together. This is still true of complex installations, but the module principle is also used in compact synthesizers. The difference is that the patchwork connections are all contained conveniently in one console, which has many control levers and knobs. However, the control panel is usually divided into a series of control sections, and a particular setting, often involving several sections, is still called a *patch.*

Interest in synthesizers grew rapidly, but at first they were so complicated and expensive that only a few studios could afford them. One of the composers making electronic music was Herbert Deutsch, of Hofstra University on Long Island. In 1963, Deutsch met engineer Robert Moog. Moog was interested in the engineering of synthesized sound, and he and Deutsch worked together to develop a small, low-cost synthesizer that could be used by both composers and performers. Electrical parts were laid out on a table and hooked to-

Herbert A. Deutsch in the Hofstra University electronic music
studio.

Robert Moog, a pioneer in the development of compact
synthesizers and components, with some of the early Moog units.

gether in various sound-making experiments. A trial
instrument was built. Twelve composers attended a
workshop to test the instrument and make suggestions.
The result was a compact instrument with practical features.

Within a few years a number of Moog synthesizers
had been purchased by composers. On the West Coast,
Donald Buchla developed a similar synthesizer, work-

ing independently with composer Morton Subotnik. Soon other synthesizers appeared, including Electro- comp, Arp, Synthi, Roland, and Korg. Instruments were being built in a number of countries, all along the lines of the first small instruments designed by Robert Moog.

During the 1960s the invention of the transistor cre- ated a revolution in electronics. In the earliest elec- tronic equipment electricity had been boosted and controlled with vacuum tubes. These tubes later were replaced by units of solid crystal materials, called *tran- sistors,* which were only a fraction of the size. The new "solid-state" elements could be grouped together closely and attached to circuit boards on which the wir- ing connections were printed or etched, rather than sol- dered to one another as they had been in the past. Eventually it became possible to integrate the compo- nents of an entire electronic circuit onto a small slice of material such as silicon, ushering in the era of space-age microelectronics.

A synthesizer is controlled by discrete amounts of electrical voltage. For example, an increase in the volt- age can make the pitch higher, while a decrease can make it lower. Other variations in voltage can be set up to make the sound loud or soft, or to change the timbre of the tones. The main source of pitch control usually is a keyboard. Each key triggers a switch to release a pre-

cise amount of voltage. This in turn controls an oscillator to produce an alternating current at a selected
frequency.

The standard synthesizer is designed for an increase
of one volt to produce a frequency or pitch one octave
higher. So to make the twelve semitones of the musical
scale, this 1-volt step is broken down into twelve
smaller steps of $\frac{1}{12}$ volt each. Suppose, for example,
the musician wants to play the melody notes for the
start of the "Star Spangled Banner," "O-oh say, can
you see. . . ." Selecting the correct intervals on the
keyboard would mean pressing half-steps, or semitones
7, 4, 0, 4, 7, and 12. These keys will release voltages of
$\frac{7}{12}$, $\frac{4}{12}$, $\frac{0}{12}$, $\frac{4}{12}$, $\frac{7}{12}$, and 1 volt. The fractional voltages
go to the oscillator, which then automatically generates
the correct pitch frequencies.

To make them economical and portable, most synthesizers have a short keyboard span. However, the
span can be greatly increased with frequency dividers,
which electronically boost or reduce the keyboard voltage exactly 1 or 2 volts to make octave jumps. On the
synthesizer these circuits are regulated by switches labeled 4', 8', 16', or 32' to match the pipe lengths of
organ terminology.

Suppose a standard organ pipe that is eight feet long
sounds the pitch of middle C on a piano when the air
inside is set into vibration. Then a pipe four feet long
will sound the pitch of C^1, one octave higher. Or a six-

teen-foot pipe will produce C_1, a tone one octave lower than that of the eight-foot pipe. And a thirty-two-foot pipe will sound C_2, two octaves lower.

The octave changes can be made alone, or sometimes blended in combinations just as they would be on a pipe organ. For instance, a single synthesizer key can play a very high note, or a note in the middle of the range, or a very low note. Or the same key can be set to trigger all three notes at the same time.

The pitch frequency of the oscillator may be con-

Moog electronic units: *(top)* the Sample and Hold note pattern generator; *(center)* a finger-touch Ribbon Controller for sliding pitches; *(bottom, left to right)* a Footswitch for changing sounds instantly; a Percussion Controller; and a variable Foot Rocker Control for making gradual changes of sound.

trolled by other means, as well. A rotating knob can be turned or a foot pedal depressed to slide the pitch up and down. There is even a type of sensitive metallic ribbon that responds to touch. As the finger moves toward one end of the ribbon the pitch rises, and as it moves toward the other end the pitch falls.

The number of oscillators in a synthesizer depends on its design and its use. All the notes of the instrument actually can be produced by only one oscillator since the frequency generated by a single oscillator can be broken down proportionately to make all twelve semitones of the scale at once. And each of these in turn can produce lower octaves through frequency dividers.

However, a synthesizer often has at least two oscillators, each one generating pitch tones. Then the player can choose sounds from oscillator number one, or oscillator number two. Suppose, for instance, oscillator number one generates sawtooth waves that sound like a trumpet, and oscillator number two generates square waves that sound like a clarinet. The player instantly can switch back and forth between the two sounds. Or by activating both oscillator switches the player can blend the sounds of the two oscillators to produce richer colors. Usually the tones of any oscillator can be adjusted so that they all come out a little higher or lower in pitch. In this way the oscillator can be tuned to match any instrument. When there are two oscillators, their pitches either can be tuned together or

tuned to different frequencies. Pressing a key then creates two pitches instead of one.

Synthesizers on which many notes can be sounded
together by pressing several keys at once are called
polyphonic, meaning "many-toned." Those that are
made for "lead" or solo use, on which only one melody
note at a time can be sounded (as with a flute, trumpet,
or other wind instrument), are called *monophonic,*
meaning "one-toned."

Basically, synthesizers produce sound frequencies
within the range of human hearing, from about 20 to
20,000 Hz. However, a synthesizer may have a second
oscillator that generates pulses at very low frequencies,
from about 0.5 to 30 Hz. This is called a *subaudio* oscillator because its frequencies are below the range of

The Korg Polysix is a polyphonic synthesizer that can play up to
six tones at once.

The Moog Opus 3, a polyphonic synthesizer, produces three basic tone groups: strings, organ, and brass. Sounds can be altered, modulated, filtered, and mixed in many combinations.

The Minimoog is a compact, three-oscillator synthesizer with basic sound-changing capabilities. It is standard among monophonic lead synthesizers.

human hearing. Its pulses are used only to modify the sound from the audio oscillator. For example, suppose the subaudio oscillator alternates at about 6 Hz. Then the pitch tone of the audio oscillator wavers slightly six times each second. The result is a vibrato like that in the human singing voice. The tone pulses and sounds "live" or "warm."

If the subaudio frequency is raised to within the lower range of human hearing, above 30–40 Hz, its combination with the high-frequency oscillation will produce clanging, gonglike sounds that can be used for unique effects.

In a synthesizer, many tonal changes can be made with electronic filters. A *filter* is a circuit that blocks certain frequencies while allowing others to pass. For instance, the sawtooth and square waves generated by most oscillators are buzzy or brilliant sounds rich in overtones. But if higher frequencies are gradually cut off through filtering, each sound becomes more mellow and flutelike. When the cutoff frequency control is changed slowly as notes are being played, the effect is a "funky" or "wah-wah" sound. It is like the change in brightness of a trumpet tone as a mute is moved in and out of the flared bell. Or if you sing "ah" as you cover and uncover your mouth with your hand, you will get a similar effect.

A filter that is more familiar is the treble tone control

on a radio. When this knob is turned all the way up, the sound is bright since all of the high frequencies are present. As the knob is turned all the way down, the high frequencies are gradually filtered out or reduced so that only the deep bass sounds remain. Rotating the knob all the way back and forth will create a similar "wah-wah" effect.

Most synthesizers also have a random noise generator. Instead of making a tone of a particular pitch, the random noise generator produces a mix of all frequencies in the audio range. This is called *white noise* and sounds like the "shhhhh" of a waterfall, or the static between stations on a radio. The random noise is used to create the sounds of cymbals, brushes on snare drums, and other percussion effects.

In tailoring synthesized sounds one more important control function is needed—the envelope generator. Just as mailing envelopes come in different shapes to surround their contents, so the envelope generator controls the overall shape, or contour, of musical sounds. It does this by regulating how the sounds start and stop, and how long they last.

Think of some familiar sounds. No two of them start and stop in exactly the same way. For example, a single drum tap will begin suddenly and end just as quickly. By contrast, a flute tone might begin more gradually and keep sounding for a long time before slowly fading away. Suppose we charted the changes in volume of the two sounds. The chart of the drum tap would look like a narrow, pointed mountain, while the chart of the flute tone would resemble a broad, flattened hill. The complete contour of these time changes in volume, or *amplitude,* is the sound envelope. It is unique to each musical instrument, and is just as important as the tonal color in characterizing its sound.

To shape the envelope, four control elements are needed: *attack time, decay time, sustain level,* and *release time.* A synthesizer will have dials or sliders to determine each of these. Attack time controls the split

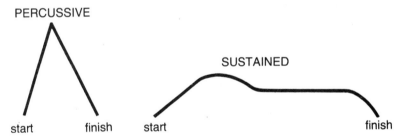

A percussive sound envelope *(left)* produces a sound that is short and explosive, with rapid rise and decay. A sustained sound envelope *(right)* produces a sound that continues like that of a wind instrument.

A = attack time
D = decay time
S = sustain
R = release time

An envelope contour.

second of time it takes for the tone to reach full volume. Decay time controls how fast the volume falls off from that point. The sustain controls at what level, if any, the tone then continues. And release time controls how rapidly the tone dies away when completed. Whenever a key is depressed, this preset information controls the resulting tone envelope. Tones with rapid attack and fast decay will sound percussive, like drums, cymbals, or plucked strings. Those with high sustain levels will sound like air-blown instruments, such as a clarinet or organ. When the envelope controls are combined with oscillator and filter controls, the command of tone quality is amazing.

An extra feature found on many synthesizers is called *sample and hold*. "Hold" means that certain electrical information is held or stored. "Sample" means that while an electrical wave is in motion a portion of it can be taken out. It is then "held" unchanging for a period of time determined by a timing clock. These samplings are used to control the musical output of a synthesizer. For example, if the up-and-down shape of a triangular wave-form is sampled, a series of rising and descending pitches would be produced. Or, if the output of a noise generator is sampled, the resulting series of notes would jump up and down in unexpected ways.

On some instruments pitch changes can be set up in advance on a row of dials. The more each dial is rotated, the higher the pitch will be. The series of preset dial tones can then be sampled by the timing clock at any speed. The sequence can form a musical background over which the musician can play a separate melody line. For instance, suppose he or she needs a simple bass pattern that repeats over and over again. Each bass note is set ahead of time with a knob marked for pitch. The timing clock then will trigger the notes in the right order. Since the performer no longer needs to play these notes, he or she can play a melody or chords on the regular keyboard above the automatic bass notes.

The synthesizer may have a digital computer memory

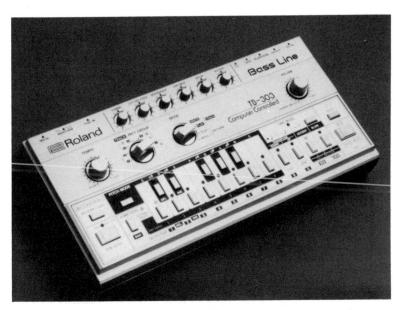

This Roland Bass Line TB-303 can be programmed to produce up to sixty-four separate bass note patterns, each with a range of three octaves. These computerized patterns can be used at any time to accompany other instruments.

for sample and hold. Suppose the digital memory can hold a series of two hundred units. First the performer presses the sample and hold button. Then he or she can play any melody that does not have more than two hundred units. The computer memory will store the melody, even keeping track of the silent spaces between notes and of how long to hold each tone. This stored melody can be played back at any speed. The performer then can add new instrument or rhythm sounds at the same time.

A magnetic tape recorder is also commonly used for storing sound patterns. With it, any recorded sequence, whether it is as short as a repeating loop of tape or as long as an extended musical composition, can be stored and played back later as needed. In actual performance live instruments can play along with a taped track of music. Or, if a special 4-track recorder is used, four parallel tracks can be independently recorded, all running in the same direction on the tape. The combined recorded sounds then can be played back together. Professional studio tape recorders can record as many as sixteen or even thirty-two parallel tracks of sound on extra-wide magnetic tape. Because tape recorders are extremely flexible in storing sound and tapes can easily be cut and spliced, several high-quality tape recorders ordinarily are used with synthesizers in composing electronic music.

Some synthesizers now have touch-sensitive keyboards that detect the speed, or *velocity*, with which a key is depressed. This is translated into variations of loud and soft, as with a piano. A second type of system detects changes in pressure while a key is held down. With this, the depressed key can be held firmly with a fingertip as the wrist is moved gently up and down. The changes in pressure create undulations in volume, making a tremolo effect. Some instruments combine both velocity- and pressure-sensitivity in their keyboard touch.

Keyboard synthesizers are so compact that a few can

The Polymoog, a touch-sensitive and fully polyphonic synthesizer, with stand and Polypedal Controller.

The Korg 80S Symphonic Piano with touch-sensitive keyboard synthesizes piano, vibes, harpsicord, clavicord, and strings. The sounds can be phase-shifted, or alternated, between speakers mounted in the console for a pulsing effect.

The Moog Liberation, a portable polyphonic synthesizer, with keyboard and controller panel. The power supply box *(right)* is mounted on a separate stand.

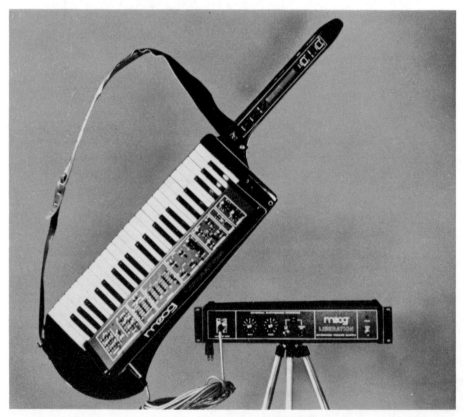

be played in completely portable style. These are carried like a guitar, supported by a strap around the neck. The single keyboard is played with one hand, like an accordion. Controls are available for either the right or the left hand. To make the instrument lighter to hold, part of the electronics is placed in a separate module mounted on a stand and connected to the keyboard module by a patch cord.

A few instruments now combine synthesized sound with electric sound. The guitar synthesizer is a good example. This instrument starts with a basic electric guitar containing the usual magnetic pickups beneath the strings. However, an extra row of six high-quality pickups, one beneath each string, is placed between the bridge and the back magnetic pickup.

Each of these six transducers delivers a signal to a separate guitar synthesizer unit. This special synthesizer has six voltage control oscillators, or VCOs. The synthesizer "follows" the changing pitches from each string individually. That is, pitches from string number one are converted to voltage changes so that matching pitches are generated by oscillator number one. Pitches from string two trigger oscillator number two, and so on. The oscillator tones then can be processed just as in any other synthesizer. Wave-forms and tone colors can be modified, and the attack and sustain envelope can be changed. Vibrato, gliding pitches and other synthesizer effects are easily added.

The Roland Guitar Controller G-202 acts as a basic electric guitar or uses a special divided pickup to isolate the sounds of individual strings and feed them to the GR-100 Electronic Guitar or the GR-300 Guitar Synthesizer.

Detail of the Guitar Controller.

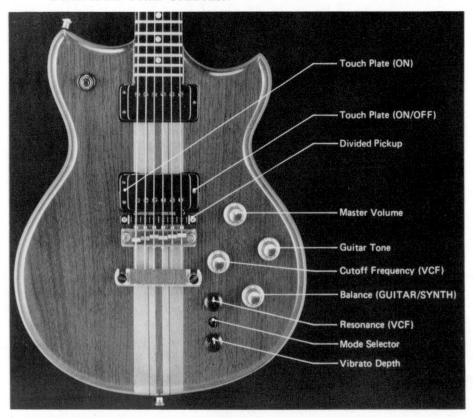

Touch Plate (ON)

Touch Plate (ON/OFF)

Divided Pickup

Master Volume

Guitar Tone

Cutoff Frequency (VCF)

Balance (GUITAR/SYNTH)

Resonance (VCF)

Mode Selector

Vibrato Depth

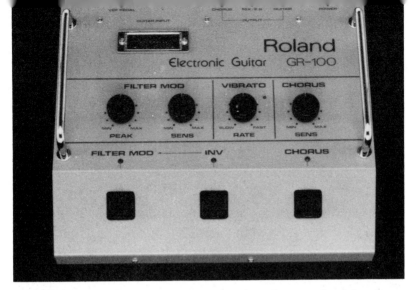

The Roland GR-100 processes, or changes, the sounds of the six strings individually. It also can add vibrato and chorus effects.

Two views of the Roland GR-300 Guitar Synthesizer. This unit uses six oscillators to change sound sources into voltage signals.

At the same time the electric signal from the regular magnetic guitar pickups is amplified in the usual way through the same unit. A balance control on the guitar can be set for either ordinary electric guitar sound, synthesized guitar sound, or any blend of the two. Some control switches are mounted on the guitar, while others are mounted on the guitar synthesizer. When this unit is on the floor, still other switches can be activated through foot buttons located along a tilted panel. The result of these combinations is an instrument that plays and handles like a guitar but also has the advantages of a synthesizer. The sounds can be like that of a guitar, but just as easily like a trumpet, a piano, an organ, or almost anything imaginable.

Another combination of synthesis with mechanically activated sound is a percussion unit produced by Mattel called Synsonic. This has four rubber pads, each taking the place of a regular drumhead. These small pads are struck with drum sticks just as the regular instruments are. However, there is no natural acoustic sound. Instead, the impulses from the sticks activate electronically synthesized sounds. Striking pad one triggers a snare drum sound. Striking pad two triggers a cymbal sound. And striking pads three and four triggers the sounds of high and low tom-toms. The small portable unit can be patched into any sound amplification system.

ELECTRONIC ORGANS

Synthesizer technology has stimulated a revolution in the design of electronic organs. Miniature circuits now make it possible for even complex organs to be manufactured at modest cost. Electronic organs are used for everything from classical music to pop, rock, and jazz. Permanent installations are built for churches and recording studios. Semiportable concert organs are made for touring recitalists. Smaller versions are found in homes and restaurants. And highly portable combo organs are carried from job to job by the pop musician.

In spite of the variety of uses for electronic organs, the basis for all of them was the sound of the classical or theater pipe organ. Electronic organs first imitated the natural sounds produced by pipe organs. Now they also imitate brass instruments, flutes and reeds, violins, harps, pianos, guitars, and percussion sounds. And like synthesizers, they can generate new sounds of their own.

Electronic organs produce tones in several basic ways. Some use a master oscillator. This generates an ultrasonic frequency far above the range of human hearing that is subdivided to create all of the notes in the normal range of the organ. Other organs use twelve separate oscillators, which produce the semitones of the highest octave of notes. Frequency dividers then create the sounds for the lower octaves. In still a third type of organ, a digital system with computer memory is used to synthesize the sounds.

Although many electronic organs have a mixture of features, there are differences between organs designed for classical sound and those used for pop and jazz music. Examples of classical organs for churches are the

The Rodgers Classic Organ combines the true sound of wind-blown pipes with electronically generated organ sounds and pedal tones. These are then amplified through speaker units located at either side of the pipe assembly and the pedalboard.

type engineered by the Rodgers Company. In the Rodgers organ there is an individual oscillator for every note of every rank. Since a *rank* is only one group of pipes with similar sounds, there are many more oscillators than there are keys and pedals.

Several methods are used to imitate the sound of real pipes electronically. For example, to duplicate the constant whistling noise of flute pipes, the Rodgers organ uses an electronic white noise generator. This makes a sound like rushing air. The noise is added to the electronic flute tones in proportion to the number of notes being sounded. In addition, the unique chirping sound, or "chiff," heard as air explodes into a pipe is imitated electronically with an effect called *flute shift*. For a split second at the start of each tone, a pitch thirty-one notes higher is added to the sound. When the rushing air and chiff effects are combined with the synthesized flute tones, the listener has a sense of real organ pipes being present in the room.

Another imitated characteristic of pipe sound is called *activity*. The tone oscillators have random fluctuations to make them purposely unsteady. The sound is then similar to a large pipe organ, in which pitches drift slightly with changing pipe combinations and variations in air supply.

Many organ customers want a true pipe organ but do not have sufficient space or cannot afford one. A compromise is to buy an organ that combines electronic sound with true pipe sound. First, several ranks of metal and wooden flue pipes are installed in the room. These are sounded with a blower at low wind pressure, as with classical organs. Then the remaining sounds of the organ, including the lowest pedal tones, are generated electronically. The amplified electronic sounds, heard through loudspeakers, are blended with those of the acoustic pipes.

Another type of church organ uses a digital computer to generate tones. This system was pioneered by the Allen Organ Company. As a preliminary step a rank of

The Allen three-manual electronic organ was designed for use in church.

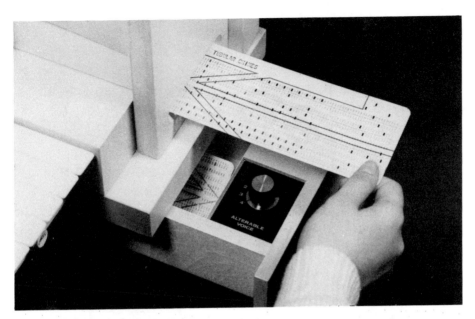

Inserting a computer card into the Allen organ to program the sound of tubular chimes. All organ sounds are generated from stored digital information.

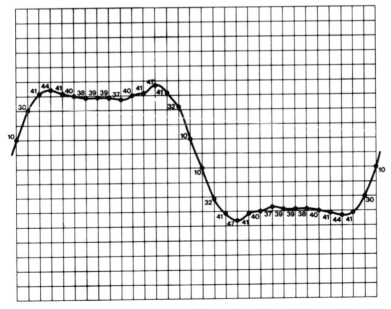

The wave-form of a "stopped" flute pipe charted in a series of numerical steps from digital computer memory.

pipes from a real pipe organ is selected to serve as a model for one particular sound, or *stop*. Suppose, for example, it is the stop labeled "Blockflute," which sounds something like a wooden recorder. One or more of the blockflute pipe sounds are tape recorded and the recording is later analyzed electronically. The wave-form of the recorded sound is converted into a series of

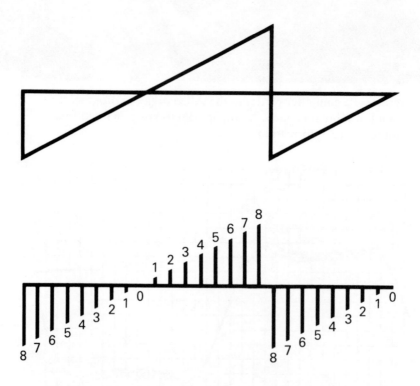

A sawtooth wave-form *(top)* is converted to digits *(bottom)*.

numbers. A computer changes the ordinary numbers into binary numbers (combinations of 1 and 0) and stores them in a digital memory. Later the player can set the organ for this sound by flipping the stop tab marked "Blockflute" to the "On" position. Then when a key is depressed, the stored sounds are recreated in a fraction of a second from the computer memory.

Some electronic organs offer special features for performing popular music. An example is the MX-1 organ, made by the Lowrey Company. It has many automated options. One of these is called "Orchestration Plus." Twelve settings are labeled for sounds ranging from "Big Band" to "Rock," "Baroque," "Disco," "Waltz," and others. By pressing a single button for the desired sound and selecting a tempo, or *time pulse,* on a slider switch, a synthesized accompaniment is heard. The Big Band setting sounds like trumpets, saxophones, trombones, and string bass, but can be switched to saxophones or brass only, or both together. As the player selects foundation tones with only one or two left-hand fingers on the lower keyboard, the accompaniment automatically changes to build matching chords based on these tones. At the same time, the note and rhythm patterns of the accompaniment also change in a variety of patterns. The effect to the listener is of a completely orchestrated big band arrangement. The other available accompaniments include mixtures of jazz guitar, classic

The Lowrey D600 MX-1 is a combination electronic organ and synthesizer, producing sounds ranging from classical to pop and jazz.

"Orchestration Plus" is one of several versatile sections of synthesized instrumental and rhythm backgrounds provided on the MX-1.

guitar, banjo, harpsichord, clarinet, accordion, fiddle, and tuba. The right hand is free to play the melody above the automated accompaniment.

A second automated section is called "Digital Stereo Rhythm." Eighteen standard rhythm backgrounds are available, such as ballad, dixie, swing, march, and waltz. At the touch of a button, brushes on cymbals, snare drums, bass, wood blocks, or other percussion sounds are synthesized to match the rhythm foundation. Introductions, solo breaks, and automatic start and stop also can be programmed with this section of the organ.

Even pitch can be altered by pressing a lever to the left of the volume pedal. If the foot is shifted to the left, the pitch is lowered or flatted. When pressure on the lever is released, the pitch returns to normal. In this way the glide of a steel guitar or slide trombone can be reproduced even while the player's hands are on the keyboard.

The MX-1 is amazingly versatile in its musical possibilities. It can be a church, theater, or jazz organ. It can sound like a big band, country band, rock, disco, or polka band. Or it can sound like a symphony or a baroque orchestra. A special section also provides sound controls like those of a lead, or solo, synthesizer. And because of the success of the programmed options on the MX-1, Lowrey now offers similar background sound and rhythm patterns available on individual com-

Lowrey's Genius Model G100, a compact console, combines basic electronic organ sounds with a variety of digitally stored background sounds programmed on interchangeable computer chips.

A digital control chip is inserted into the Genius console.

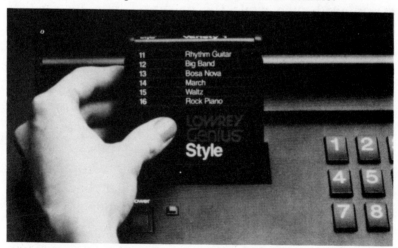

puter chips that can easily be added to a less expensive instrument called the Genius.

A number of companies make portable electronic organs for nightclub work. The Hammond B-200 is a good example. The keyboard console is mounted on supports and can be detached. The one-octave pedalboard also is detachable from the base frame. The organ's speakers are in a separate cabinet on rollers. All of the modules can be transported from place to place in a van.

The basic wave-form of the combo organ is a square wave, producing a clear percussive or clarinetlike sound. The square waves are combined or filtered to create a wide variety of colors, from string to brass, reed, and flute. The filtered flutelike sounds, or sine waves, can be combined with sliding drawbars to produce the traditional Hammond sound. A special group of stops, used on certain models, is called "Brite Percussion." This group combines various octaves of the square waves to create sounds like piano, harpsichord, guitar, and vibes. These sounds are all short or explosive. However, when they are sustained, they then resemble clarinet, trumpet, oboe, or other instruments whose sounds can be held at a constant level.

The combo organ connects to a separate speaker system designed by the Leslie Company. A unique sound is achieved by rotating the speaker elements at selected speeds. For the highest tones, small twin speakers are set into rotation. For the lower tones there is a rotating drum with a hollowed-out curve inside. The speaker is positioned upside down above the drum. When the drum rotates, the hollow curve directs the sound to one side, sweeping the sound around in a circle. The sound literally fills the room and seems to pulse with a pleasant undulation. Rotating speakers now are used with many types of organs, from home and combo to church. They are one way of adding to the electronic organ some of the sense of space found in pipe organs installed in large auditoriums.

SOUND PROCESSORS

Sound processors alter sounds electronically in many ways. For instance, specific units can filter out certain frequencies, distort, pulsate, or multiply a single sound, or generate artificial echoes. Some of these sound-processing elements are built right into synthesizers or electronic organs; others are manufactured as independent units that can be patched into almost any sound system. Due to solid-state technology, the modules, or *boxes,* are compact and convenient. The devices usually have knobs, foot pedals, or switches so that they can be controlled easily during a performance.

The various electronic sound processors are now so widely used that they all are part of the popular sound of today's music.

MXR sound processors include a DynaComp volume compressor, Phaser, Stereo Flanger, Stereo Chorus, Distortion Plus fuzz unit, and a Time Delay echo-and-reverberation unit.

Envelope Filter • One popular sound processor is the *frequency envelope filter*. It cuts off the high frequencies of the sound in a flexible way. The device is sensitive to the volume of the incoming sound. The louder the sound, the higher the cutoff frequency; the softer the sound, the lower the cutoff frequency. The brightness of the sound then changes right along with the volume, creating an automatic "wah-wah" effect that exactly follows whatever music is being played. For instance, when there are sustained melody notes with sharp attack, each tone starts out bright and suddenly turns mellow. The resulting sound is called funky.

Phaser • Another useful device is the phase shifter, or *phaser*. This electrically shifts the peaks of identical sound wave-forms slightly out of synchronization. The sounds are alternately canceled and reinforced, creating an effect something like that of rotating loudspeakers. The sound seems to pulse and shift almost as if it were moving around in the room. Usually there are adjustments for both speed and intensity.

Flanger • A unit similar to the phaser is called the *flanger*. The name comes from the flange, or outer rim, of a reel of recording tape. Suppose two reels of tape are placed on two different recorders, each playing the same sound at the same time. If you slow one reel down by dragging a thumb against the flange, its sound will become lower in pitch than that from the reel on the other machine. By alternately pressing and releasing the thumb, a "wow-wow" or undulation will be created in the combined sound. This is *flanging*. In a modern flanging unit the same effect is accomplished electronically.

Chorus • The *chorus unit* makes a single sound source seem like a group. One singer can be made to sound like two or more similar voices, all singing the same melody. Or one string sound from a synthesizer can sound like an orchestral section of strings. For the chorus effect the sound source is divided into two chan-

The MXR Envelope Filter is triggered by the volume of incoming sound to produce a "wah-wah," or funky, effect.

This Boss Flanger BF-2 electronically produces the "wow-wow" effect caused by slowing the outer rim, or flange, of a reel of recording tape.

A chorus unit, such as this Boss Chorus CE-2, produces the effect of multiple voices from one sound input.

nels. The first channel passes the sound unchanged. The second channel alters the pitch slightly. This signal is recombined with the original sound, creating the slight mistuning that occurs naturally when several instruments play the same melody. There is still actually only one sound. But it now seems multiplied, as if various performers were playing almost, but not quite exactly, together. This is so like what actually happens with a group of players that the effect of a chorus can be quite convincing.

Distortion Unit • Another kind of processor puts distortion into the sound. Sometimes this happens at a live concert when the music is too loud for the sound system to handle. It begins to sound noisy or buzzy. The loud distortion becomes part of the excitement of the concert, but it is hard on the equipment and hard on the ears of the listeners. With a *distortion unit* this same exciting effect is duplicated at safer listening levels. When the electronic distortion is extreme, the effect is called *fuzz*, which is a very good description of the sound. And so a distortion unit often is called a *fuzz box*.

Rhythm Sequencer • Many compact units now create rhythms electronically. They are literally "rhythm boxes." Some use a random noise oscillator. Others use computers to store percussion sounds digitally, much like the Allen organ. A typical unit will have programmed sounds such as bass, snare drums, brushes on cymbal, high-hat cymbals, tom-toms, conga drums, bongos, woodblock, claves (sticks), tambourine, and cowbell. Either a two-beat or a three-beat rhythm can be chosen. Speed can be adjusted with a knob or sliding control.

Besides the regular rhythm patterns, the rhythm sequencer can also produce rolls or other introductions, as well as short percussion solos called *bridges* to be used between longer song sections. These can be set up ahead of time and flipped in and out with a foot switch or panel control. Some percussion units can store several complete rhythm sequence patterns that will play for an entire song.

Reverberation/Echo • One of the most useful sound processors generates both artificial reverberation and echo. Such a unit uses electronic storage to delay the incoming signal, and then recombines it at a lower volume level with the original signal. The result is direct sound plus delayed sound. If there is enough time between the direct and delayed sounds, the original sound seems to repeat like a machine gun. But if the time delays overlap and drop off in volume, the sound duplicates the natural echoes of a large hall. This is called *reverberation*, and the time it takes for the reflected or delayed sound to die away is called *reverberation time*.

Mixer • Sometimes there are many sound processing units and many instruments all being used together. Then still one more device is needed to handle the connections. This is called a *mixer*. Mixers come in various sizes, but all do the same job—combining or blending the electrical signals from the separate sources.

A mixer will have a series of both input jacks to patch in various signal sources and output jacks to patch the mixed signals to sound processors or amplifiers. For example, a patch cord from an electric piano might be plugged into one input. The cord from a voice mike might go to another input, and that from a synthesizer to still another. Each input will have its own set of controls. On a typical mixer panel these might include: VOL, TON, REV, PAN, and EFF. These are all ab-

Roland's PA-150 Stereo Mixing Amp combines eight-channel sound mixing with basic amplification.

breviations. The knob marked "VOL" controls the volume from that input. "TON" is the tone control. "REV" means that the mixer itself can add reverberation to sustain the sound. "PAN" means that the balance of sound can be "panned," or shifted, between two loudspeakers by turning the control to the left or right. And "EFF" stands for "effects." This knob controls a connection from the mixer to any other sound-processing unit whose output is fed back to the mixer, thus altering the sound. It could be a "wah-wah" box, a phaser, a chorus, or a fuzz box.

By adjusting the separate rows of knobs, the performer can balance or change the individual inputs. A guitar solo can be made louder. A synthesizer can be

dropped down to background level. Echo or reverberation can be added to a singer's voice. Or other effects
can be added or taken away. The sound is being engineered electronically just as in a recording studio. The
"mixed" sound then is patched into a separate amplifier
and speaker system.

Since a mixer can use inputs from ordinary microphones as well as electronic sources, it actually can
combine the sounds of acoustic instruments with those
of electric and electronic instruments. Whether the
original sounds are soft or loud, bright or mellow, a
pleasing mix can be achieved.

3

PREFORMING
AND RECORDING
ELECTRONIC MUSIC

COMPOSERS, PERFORMERS, AND SOUND STUDIOS

The development of electronic instruments and music
has brought together many skills that were once iso-
lated. In the past usually a composer wrote music, a
performer played it, and an engineer recorded it. But
these distinctions are starting to disappear. To begin
with, the task of performing on today's electronic keyboards is not a simple one. Previously, the keyboard
player used one instrument, usually a piano. Today's
keyboard performer, however, might be called on to
use an electric piano, a combo organ, and a string synthesizer, all during the same performance. The instru-

75

ments are placed at easy-to-reach angles to one another or simply stacked vertically on a rack.

The player must still have a basic keyboard technique. But he or she also must understand the settings and capabilities of the various electronic instruments, as well as how to tailor their sounds and patch them through various pieces of equipment so that the resulting amplified sounds are correct and in proper balance. In short, the player must be something of an acoustical and electronic engineer as well as a keyboard technician.

If the performing group has many electronic sound sources and is successful enough professionally, an extra member may be given the job of setting, controlling, and altering the sounds during an entire performance. Although this member is not a performer, he or she must fully understand the music in order to make adjustments that will help convey it to the listener.

Various members of any group will need to know how to handle recording equipment. Even making a simple home demo tape may require recording separate tracks on a 4-track machine. This will mean recording one or two tracks at a time and then listening to the recorded tracks through one earphone while adding new sounds on the remaining tracks. The procedure calls for some of the same skills normally used by a studio recording engineer.

Or suppose one member of a group wants to com-

The Casiotone 7000 is a stereo keyboard with multitrack composing capabilities.

pose a new song. He or she might use a programmed percussion sequencer or electric bass sequencer for the background. The percussion part must not only be composed but set up, button by button, on the electronic unit. And all changes in the bass line must be similarly programmed. Then perhaps the player will add voice and keyboard at the same time, making tonal changes on the keyboard during the process. And all of the sounds are patched into the channels of a 4-track tape machine. This kind of one-person operation is not unusual today, and the person who can combine such skills has a definite advantage.

Another technical area important to a composer today is computer science. Much of the growth of electronic music, both in composing and recording, has followed the development of this new science. For example, one of the first purely computer compositions was made in the 1950s by Lejaren Hiller working at the University of Illinois. The composer had a background in both music and engineering. The computer, named after the university, was called the Illiac. It was programmed in advance with a set of rules about the form the music was to take. Although these basic rules could not be broken, they did allow for many variations. The computer memory held a bank of musical notes stored in a mathematical code.

The Illiac sampled the coded notes at random. Any notes could come up in any order, but only certain arrangements of notes fit the programmed rules. These patterns were used to fill in the form of the composition, while those notes that did not fit the rules were rejected. The resulting computer printout was converted to conventional musical notation and performed later by a string quartet. It was named the *Illiac Suite*.

Most of today's electronic music studios involve experiments with computer control programs, composition, storage, and printout. Programs, called *software*, now are offered for composing music and can be used with home office computers. For instance, music writing programs are available for the Apple computer. The Apple system consists of several floppy disk machines, a control typewriter, and a TV display screen.

Amplifier and speakers can be connected to the setup.

Basic musical information, such as a music staff, notes, rests, and other musical designations, has been prerecorded in digital form on a floppy disk. When the basic disk is played, the preselected musical symbols are displayed on the TV screen. With control knobs, pointers are moved to different positions on the screen to select the musical elements one by one, just as the composer would write them on a piece of paper. These are recorded digitally on another floppy disk.

Preprogrammed tone selections can be chosen for the various sound tracks, or *voices,* of the composition. Or a grid can be displayed on the screen. Then, any wave-form like that of an existing musical instrument can be built and stored by the computer. Or a new wave-form can be created that will produce a sound never heard before. These new wave-forms and corresponding sounds can then be used in addition to the basic programmed sounds. At any time parts of the stored musical composition can be played back through the amplifier and speaker system. Elements can be erased, revised, or stored permanently on the floppy disk.

Certain computerized electronic musical instrument keyboards, such as the Rhodes Chroma or the Synclavier, also can be connected directly to the Apple computer. Music performed on the keyboard can then be stored digitally by the computer on a floppy disk. And as with the music writing system, this stored infor-

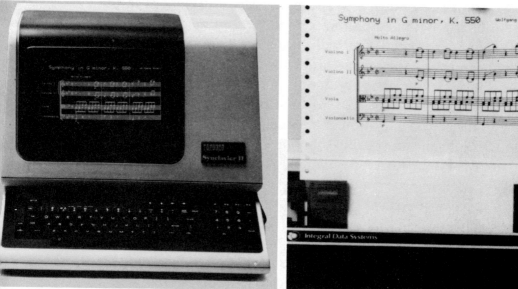

This Synclavier II system combines a synthesizer keyboard with digital memory *(top)*, a control terminal with display screen for converting stored sounds to music symbols *(left)*, and a computer printer producing a finished sheet of music notation *(right)*.

mation can be converted to sounds played through the attached amplifier and speaker system.

Performers and composers who do studio recording may use highly complex electronic equipment, costing many thousands of dollars. But this certainly is not always the case. There are many electronic instruments whose prices range from under $100 to not more than $1000. Because of advances in technology even the least expensive of these can offer amazing quality for the money. A good performer can get such excellent results from a $600 keyboard that listeners would be convinced that $6000 worth of equipment must be on hand. And an ingenious composer with only a simple basement setup can make a master tape for a disk recording that may be better than most tapes coming out of huge professional studios. This is possible because even one modest synthesizer can be used for multiple recording, becoming its own orchestra and creating as many individual or grouped sounds as are needed.

Electronic music is used increasingly in commercial recordings because the producer can save money. Say, for example, that the background music for a half-hour TV film is to be recorded. The producer must not only pay the studio engineers for making the recording, but must also pay the individual musicians for their time. If the score calls for the sound of a full orchestra, this might require eight violins, four violas, two cellos, and a string bass in the string section alone. To save money

This Roland Studio System includes various synthesizer, control, and special effects modules.

the producer can hire only one violinist, one violist, one cellist, and so on, and duplicate the extra instruments on a synthesizer with chorus effects or multiple track recording. The result will be somewhat like the sound of a whole section of each instrument. Or suppose that only electronic sounds are needed. One good studio musician who is thoroughly familiar with the equipment can do all of the recording for an entire TV film.

A good example of the mixture of skills needed in quality recording is the preparation of the score for the Walt Disney feature film *Tron*, a fantasy about a futuristic computer universe, released in 1982. The sound track combines the music of a real orchestra with an unusual variety of taped sound effects, and purely electronic synthesizer music and effects. The musical score was developed by Wendy Carlos, a New York musician with a background in keyboard and composition.

Sessions were held in England in Royal Albert Hall to record the orchestral parts on separate tape tracks to isolate individual instruments or instrumental groups. Pipe organ parts were individually recorded there as well. Later in her own electronic music and recording studio in New York, Carlos selected parts from the orchestra and organ tapes and blended them with sounds produced on an electronic synthesizer. The vocal chorus parts, recorded in California by the UCLA Chorus, were blended with orchestra and synthesizer sounds using multiple track recorders and special electronic mixing and control equipment.

At the same time on the West Coast synthesist Frank Sarafine began making a library of sound effects for the film. Ordinary sounds with unusual qualities, including the grinding of a Goodyear blimp propeller and the motor noises inside a refrigerator, were captured on magnetic tape. Electronic sounds from the computer chips used for video games were added to the collection, and synthesizers like the Minimoog, Prophet-5, and Fairlight were used to create a library of special electronic effects. An Atari computer then cataloged the sounds and stored them on reels of 16-track tape.

Later, two edited recordings were made—one for the original soundtrack album, and a slightly different one with more tape and electronic effects for the actual film.

Only the combination of professionals involved in the project, bringing together their skills of musicianship, engineering, and editing, could have created the final product.

BUYING YOUR OWN ELECTRONIC INSTRUMENTS

To make electronic music you will need to be as good a musician as if you were to peform on a piano, violin, or trumpet. There is no substitute for learning how to read and write music, and how to use your fingers properly on a keyboard or other instrument. But provided that you already know some basics about playing an acoustic piano, guitar, or bass, you can easily learn how to select your own instruments and setups, and to get good results from synthesizers, electronic organs, electric pianos, and electric guitars and basses.

If you want to look for an electronic instrument, along with some processing and amplifying equipment, keep these pointers in mind when shopping. First, be sure of your budget limitations. You do not need to buy everything all at once. Before buying anything, try as many kinds of instruments as you can get your hands on. If you have friends who already own and play electronic instruments, ask them to show you how they work. Try the instrument at your friend's house, or perhaps you can borrow it for a short time if you agree to be responsible for any damage. If you have a chance to listen to a professional group in which one of the members plays an instrument you like, don't hesitate to go up to ask about the instrument after the program. The performer will probably be pleased that you are interested and can show you several features at first hand, or may even let you play the instrument briefly.

Find teachers in your area who are competent on the instruments that interest you. They may teach in a music store, studio, or at home. Ask them which instruments they consider the best and easiest to use. Find out from teachers, professionals, and friends what they have paid for their instruments. You will begin to get an idea of what the fair values are, and of course you may learn of some good sources for purchase.

Check the newspaper ads in the classified section. Most papers have a separate category for used musical instruments. There is a rapid turnover in electronic musical instruments, simply because most performers must start with lower-priced instruments and then upgrade or expand their equipment gradually. Used items may be almost as good as new ones, depending on how they have been handled and how long they have been used. If you find a used instrument that is reasonably priced and seems in good condition, ask a professional or teacher to check it out for you before you buy it.

If you plan to purchase your instrument new, make sure you have some idea of its real value before you buy it. Do comparison shopping. Some stores will give you a price over the phone. Others require you to come in. Simply drop in, ask for the price, and then go on to the next store. Go back to the stores where the prices are fair and where you think you will get proper attention. Every store has a reputation, and teachers and professionals can help steer you to the most reliable places.

Once you have decided on a music store instrument, always ask for a full demonstration and a chance to try the instrument to your satisfaction. Some stores will even specify a trial period during which you can return the instrument for a full refund if you do not like it. Find out if the store you are buying the instrument from has such a policy. Before you do actually purchase a new instrument, make sure it is covered by a guarantee. Ask about servicing in case it should need repair in the future.

PLAYING ELECTRONIC INSTRUMENTS

Competition among the manufacturers of electronic musical instruments increases constantly, and there is an almost endless selection of excellent equipment. The following list of instruments and devices, along with operating suggestions, includes basic categories that you will probably be most interested in. All of these instruments and units are priced from around $100 to less than $1000, making them suitable for home, school, or other use. All will produce quality sounds. There are many similar instruments and devices of comparable quality, each offering its own unique features, and these step-by-step tips should serve as useful examples to help you get started in achieving good results from any of them.

Gibson ES-355 Electric Guitar • The ES-355 is typical of many electric guitars that have two sets of pickups, or transducers, beneath the strings. It is an acoustic–electric instrument, so only modest sound comes directly from the steel strings, and must be amplified electronically. The ES-355 will connect to the guitar or instrument input of any large amplifier and speaker system, although a small 10- or 15-watt guitar amp with its own built-in speaker is perfectly adequate for a moderate-sized room.

In matching any instrument to an amp it is a good rule for both the volume control on the instrument and the amplifier volume control to be set neither extremely high nor extremely low. The amplifier needs to receive a signal strong enough to handle, but not so strong that it overloads the input stage. On the other hand, if the input signal is so weak that the amp must be turned all the way up, distortion will be added in the final stages of amplification.

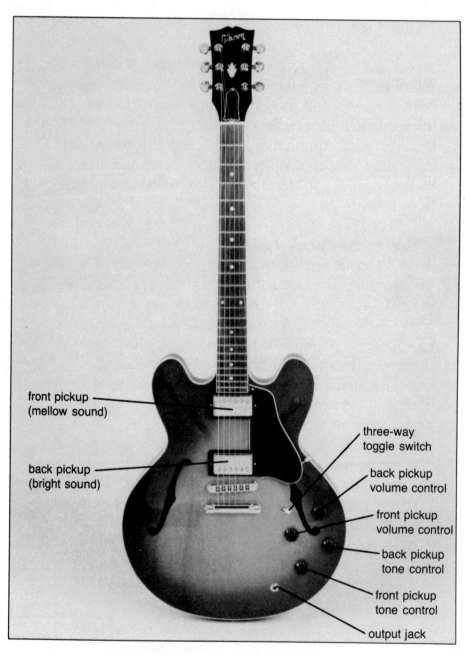

front pickup
(mellow sound)

back pickup
(bright sound)

three-way
toggle switch

back pickup
volume control

front pickup
volume control

back pickup
tone control

front pickup
tone control

output jack

The Gibson ES-355 Electric Guitar.

Sound vibrations emanating from the loudspeaker can activate the pickups on the guitar, causing a feedback howl. To avoid this, place yourself either beside the amplifier or slightly behind it, with the amp speaker pointing in the same direction as the guitar. With this positioning the sound will be louder to listeners in front of the speaker than it is to you. To create the right sound level you will have to get used to hearing yourself at a lower level than you think is right.

Plug in the patch cord from the guitar to the amp before turning on the amplifier. This will avoid unwanted pops and noises. Set all guitar volume and tone controls to mid-position and the amp volume to "0." Turn on the amp and then rotate the volume control to a comfortable listening level.

Set the guitar's three-way toggle switch to mid-position. Play test notes and chords on the guitar with the regular plastic plectrum. Flip the toggle switch up. Only sounds detected by the "front" pickup will be heard, producing a mellow sound from its location near the middle of the strings. Now flip the toggle switch down. Only sounds detected by the "back" pickup will be heard, producing a bright, metallic sound from its position near the bridge. Then return the toggle switch to mid-position, blending the sound from both pickups so it is both clear and full at the same time.

Adjust the back and front pickup volume controls to produce contrasts between mellow and edgy tones, and changes of balance in the blended sound. Make similar adjustments with the amplifier tone and volume controls. In general, it is best to set the amp for adequate treble response and then make all other adjustments from the guitar, since the tones never can be made brighter than the amp setting will allow. Remember to keep the volume a little lower than what sounds right to you, since you should not be directly in front of the speaker.

The sounds of an electric guitar tend to be rather pure and mellow. This is particularly true of the bass strings, which must have flat or polished windings that will not squeak when your left-hand fingers shift along them. Therefore, tone settings that produce bright and clear sounds will eliminate the problem of muddy-sounding bass or chords, and usually will be the most successful both in playing solo or joining with other instruments. A light right- and left-hand playing action is then sufficient to make all the sounds clear to the listener. With an electric guitar it never is necessary to force the tones, since the volume settings can be adjusted as needed.

Gibson Victory Artist Bass • Since this Gibson instrument is an electric bass guitar, it has features similar to the Gibson ES-355 Electric Guitar. There are four strings with a fretted fingerboard, and two electromagnetic pickups anchored on the solid body beneath the strings.

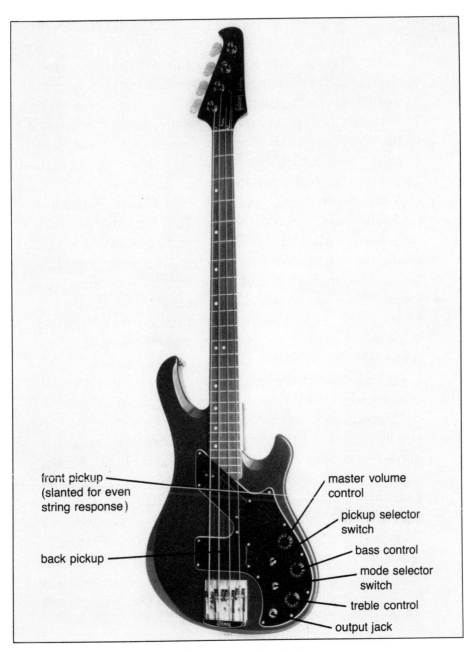

front pickup
(slanted for even
string response)

back pickup

master volume
control

pickup selector
switch

bass control

mode selector
switch

treble control

output jack

The Gibson Victory Artist Bass, with 9-volt battery.

The one nearer the center of the strings detects a very mellow sound, while the one nearest the bridge detects a slightly brighter sound. A patch cord connects the bass to any heavy-duty amplifier and speaker designed to handle bass guitar. There is a separate volume control for each pickup, and a single treble and single bass control for all guitar sound.

A three-way toggle switch controls pickup input. One position activates only the back pickup, one position only the front pickup, and the middle position a blend of the two. A second toggle switch, the mode selector, further refines the sound. The forward position activates a "passive" mode that reduces treble and bass response, the back position activates normal "active" response, and the mid-position reduces the volume of mid-range frequencies.

As with the electric guitar, you must position yourself beside or behind the amplifier speakers to avoid a feedback howl, and the bass sound will not seem as loud to you as it does to the listener. The electric bass usually is played one tone at a time, the player plucking the strings by alternating the first finger on the right hand with the second and third fingers held together for added volume. Except for occasional solos, the bass is a foundation or supporting instrument, using both regular and syncopated, or offbeat, rhythms. As a general rule, volume levels should be low and tone settings bright to avoid muddy sound and to keep the pitches and rhythms absolutely clear.

Roland's Piano Plus 70, a touch-sensitive keyboard, produces sounds of a piano, harpsichord, and clavichord. The unit has internal speakers, or it can be patched to an outside amplifier-speaker system.

Roland Piano Plus 70 • This Roland electronic piano has a span of seventy-five keys, more than many combo instruments and enough to play most piano music without worrying about missing bass or treble notes. It also has its own built-in amplifier and two speakers, one at each end of the piano. The keyboard unit fits into a carrying case and weighs only about twenty-five pounds, making it easily portable. The keyboard can be placed on any flat surface, or can be rested on the tubular stand available with the instrument.

The volume from the internal speakers will be sufficient for an average-sized room. Plug the electrical cord into a wall socket. Set the keyboard volume, sustain, and touch knobs to mid-position. Press the "On" switch.

There are four preset tone colors available at the push of a button: "Piano I," "Piano II," "Harpsichord I," and "Harpsichord II." The basic piano sound, and the most mellow tone, is obtained by the Piano I setting. Press the button labeled Piano I. A tiny red light shows when the button is on. Play any piano music. Notice that the sounds die away somewhat quickly after each key is depressed. Rotate the sustain knob from "½" toward "¾" position. The tones will gradually sustain a little longer before dying away until they closely match the sustain of an acoustic piano. More sustain than this will produce an organlike effect. Less sustain will produce the drier effect of a lute or a harp as sounds die away quickly. Unless you want either of these more extreme effects, return the sustain to ¾ position.

The Piano Plus 60 offers similar features in a more compact keyboard.

Press Piano II. The sound will change from a mellow piano to a bright one. Try pressing the buttons for Harpsichord I and Harpsichord II. The sounds get progressively thinner, brighter, and more percussive.

These four tone settings provide a complete range of changes. However, buttons can also be pressed in combination. For example, press Piano I and Harpsichord II and release the buttons together so that both stay down at the same time. The sounds will now be a combination of the two settings, with a pleasant bell-like quality that is both mellow and crisp at the same time. Pressing both Piano I and Piano II will produce a tone that seems in between the two settings. It is not as mellow as Piano I alone, nor as bright as Piano II alone. Any two or more settings can be combined in this way.

The Roland Piano Plus 70 also has a chorus setting. Pressing this button adds a blended or slightly shimmering spatial effect to the tone settings already in use, as if the tones have been multiplied, or you were playing in a larger room. Just as with a regular piano, the Roland has a foot sustain pedal. Position the sustain box on the floor about where it would be on an acoustic piano. Plug the cord into the back of the Roland at the input marked "Pedal." Pressing the pedal now sustains the sound even when the fingers are lifted from the keys.

The Piano Plus 70 has a touch-sensitive keyboard. Striking a key more rapidly or vigorously produces a louder sound than when the key is struck gently. The change is noticeable, but not as great as that on an acoustic piano. Touch response also can be varied through the knob marked "Touch." Tones start more softly when the knob is rotated to the left and more loudly when the knob is rotated to the right.

For quiet practicing, you can use a set of earphones, either those available with the instrument or any set of high-fidelity ones. Simply plug in the earphone cord jack at the input at the back marked "Phone." This automatically cuts off sound from the internal speakers and channels it through the headset. No one else in the room can hear the music.

The Keyboard Plus also has outputs for either one or two cords to be patched to an external amplifier. This can be a Roland piano amplifier or any other amplification system with a standard low impedence mike input. Volume to the amp is controlled either with a three-position switch at the back of the keyboard or with the regular keyboard volume knob. Sounds then will be heard from both the internal and the outside amp speakers.

Casiotone MT-40 • This synthesizer is a compact combo keyboard with thirty-seven black and white keys and an additional octave of bass keys. There are twenty-two tone selections and automatic rhythm settings. The tones and rhythms are synthesized electronically. The

The Casio MT-40 keyboard has twenty-two individual tone colors, an octave of bass sounds, automatic rhythms, and a self-contained battery and speaker.

light, portable unit has its own built-in speaker with enough volume for a small room.

To operate the MT-40 you can either use the unit's internal batteries or plug its A.C. adapter cord into a wall socket. Start with the volume and tempo knobs set to mid-position. Press the "On" switch. For any particular piece of music you are going to play you can choose up to four of the twenty-two tone colors in advance.

Position the "Mode" switch at "Set." Position the "Tone Memory" switch at "1." Notice that each white key has an individual tone setting marked just above it. Normally each white key plays its own pitch note, but with the Mode switch at Set, the keys temporarily become tone selector switches. Touch any white key. You will hear the sound labeled above it, and the tone memory will store it as selection 1. You can change your mind as many times as you like, because only the last sound chosen will be stored. Once you have selected tone number one, shift the Tone Memory switch to "2." Choose another white-key tone setting. Continue the process to select sounds three and four, then set the Mode switch to "Play." The synthesizer now has four separate sound choices stored in tonal memory.

Using the control labeled "Preset," you now can switch instantly among the four chosen tone settings as you play. Suppose you have picked "Trumpet," "Funny Fuzz," "Flute," and "String Ensemble." Slide the preset lever to position "1." Play anything on the keyboard and it will sound like a trumpet. Quickly shift the lever to position "4." Immediately everything you play will sound like a string ensemble. If you are playing the keyboard with only your right hand, you even can shift tone settings as you play by using your free left hand. The MT-40 is polyphonic so that up to eight keys can be activated at once with both hands for full chords as well as melodies.

Now suppose you wish to add an automatic rhythm to the keyboard music. Set the "Rhythm" slider switch to "Waltz," "Samba," "Swing," "Slow Rock," "Pops," or "Rock." Press the "Rhythm Start" button and adjust the "Tempo" knob to speed up or slow down the pulse of the rhythm you have selected. It now sounds as if a rhythm section is accompanying you in just the style and tempo you have chosen. Simply add the regular keyboard sounds to the automatic accompaniment, using either one or both hands.

You can further expand your "combo" to include the sounds of deep bass. Continue to play the regular keys with your right hand as you shift your left hand to the small bass keys at the left. The bass tones will sound like electric bass or the pedal notes of an electronic organ. The right hand tone colors will contrast with those of the deep bass just as if two instruments were playing instead of one. The Casio also will provide partly automatic bass. Press the button marked "Casio Bass." Now as you press a single bass key that matches the chord notes you are playing with the right hand, the synthesizer will automatically provide a fill-in pattern of alternating bass notes.

Two more effect controls are included on the MT-40. One is "Vibrato," which adds an undulating pulse to the sounds. The other is "Sustain," which allows the sounds to overlap for an echo or reverberation effect.

For a compact, low-cost instrument, the MT-40 is extremely versatile, actually generating sounds that imitate a small combo of instruments playing together.

Like most other electronic keyboards, the MT-40 has an input for a headphone. It also has a provision for a patch cord to an outside unit. This is marked "Line Out," and can be connected directly to the line input of a tape recorder or the auxiliary input of any hi-fi amplifier or receiver. Since the internal speaker of the MT-40 is very small, the bass tones are most effective when heard through a larger speaker system.

Yamaha CS-01 Monophonic Synthesizer • Although small and inexpensive, the Yamaha CS-01 is a true synthesizer with many of the most important basic controls and functions. It has thirty-two black and white keys, making two and one-half octaves of notes, but its range can be greatly expanded through special settings. It runs on either six "AA" batteries or uses an AC adapter to plug into a wall socket. The instrument is not only portable for tabletop use but also includes a strap so that it can hang from the shoulder like a guitar. A small amplifier and tiny speaker are built into the unit, but it also can be patched into any larger amplification system for full sound use.

All the slider controls of the CS-01 are arranged neatly across the top panel above the keyboard. First, rotate the "Power/Volume" knob at the left of the keyboard all the way to number 10. This turns on the synthesizer and sets a good listening level.

The top panel is divided into sections marked from left to right LFO, VCO, VCF, VCA, and EG. Make certain that the LFO slider is at "S" and the "Modulation" wheel is at "0." Start with the VCO section. This is the *voltage control oscillator*. It generates the synthe-

The Yamaha CS-01 Micro Monophonic Synthesizer keyboard with LFO, VCO, VCF, VCA, and Envelope Contour sections.

sizer's basic tones. One of the VCO sliders is marked "Wave." Pictured along this slider from top to bottom are five settings: triangular wave, sawtooth wave, square wave, rectangular wave, and PWM, which stands for "Pulse Width Modulation."

Set the Wave slider knob at the triangular wave. To the left of the Wave slider are three other sliders. Set these and all remaining sliders in the sections marked VCF, VCA, and EG as shown in Diagram A. Now de-

DIAGRAM A

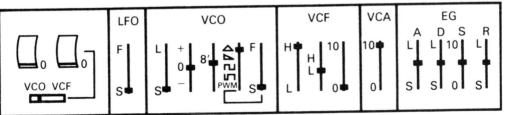

Basic panel settings on the Yamaha CS-01 synthesizer.

press any key. Notice that the sound is a little like a flute or recorder. Switch the Wave slider to the sawtooth wave position. The tone will become more brilliant, like that of a brass instrument. Try the settings for square wave and rectangular wave and notice how the tone changes to a clarinetlike sound.

With the VCO slider marked "Feet" the pitch tones can be shifted up or down in jumps of an octave. Suppose, for example, you are playing C, the fifth white key from the left. When you switch the slider from 8' to 4' the tone will jump up one octave to the next higher C. When you switch from 8' to 16' the tone will jump down an octave, and when you switch to 32' the tone will jump down still one more octave. The numbers come from the traditional lengths of organ pipes as described in Chapter 2. With these octave settings the total range of the instrument becomes five and one-half octaves, which is like having fifty-six keys to play instead of just thirty-two.

Now you are ready to further control the basic tones you have selected with the VCO by using the panel section labeled EG, for *envelope generator*. It has sliders labeled "Attack Time," "Decay Time," "Sustain Time," and "Release Time." Press any key over and over again as you move the Attack Time slider slowly between "L" and "S." At L the tones begin very gently, almost like a moan or a soft sigh. As the slider moves toward S the tones begin more and more sharply, like a drum or a guitar. Return the slider to mid-position.

Now move the Decay Time slider slowly between L and S while you press a key repeatedly. As the slider moves toward S the tones sound less and less abrupt or percussive. Return the Decay Time slider to mid-position.

The Sustain Time slider is marked "10" and "0." With the slider at 0 there is no effect on the tone at all. However, as the slider moves toward 10 the tone becomes more and more sustained, or organlike, as long as a key is still held down.

The release time slider controls how quickly the tone dies away after the key is released. As the slider moves from L to S, the tone seems to hang over longer and longer after the key is released.

Next, familiarize yourself with the VCF section. This is the *voltage control filter*. The slider on the left is a simple frequency cutoff. "H" stands for "high" and "L" for "low." When the slider is at H, all of the sound generated by the VCO and shaped by the EG is allowed to come through and the tones are at their brightest. However, as the slider is moved toward L, the higher frequencies gradually are blocked so that the sound becomes more and more mellow. After trying this, return the slider to H so that the next step will be most effective.

The "Resonance" slider in the VCF section has only two switch positions. In the "H" position there is a slight resonance effect. In the "L" position there is a more definite change as the tone becomes brassy or penetrating. This is because the highest frequencies passed by the Frequency Cutoff filter are emphasized by being fed back immediately into the tone.

With the remaining slider, "EG Depth," the settings from the EG section can be added to the VCF section. For example, a sharp attack setting at 10 can make the start of each tone brighter than its sustained sound to create a modern "funky" effect.

The VCA section, or *voltage control amplifier*, has one slider. Settings from both the VCF section and the EG section automatically are fed to the VCA. The total sound intensity then can be regulated with the VCA slider.

Several other controls are included to modify the synthesizer sounds even further. Let's say you want to duplicate a fast run. Simply use the "Glissando" slider at the left of the VCO section. Then, when two keys far apart are pressed in succession, all of the in-between notes will also be heard slowly or rapidly, one by one. Or suppose you want wavering or pulsing effects. One way to create them is to move the "Pitch Blend" wheel by hand to raise or lower the pitch gradually. When you let go of the wheel, it will return to normal position. Or you can set the "Modulation" switch to VCO and rotate the "Modulation" wheel gradually away from 0. A slow pulse generated by the LFO, or *low frequency os-*

cillator, now will create a regular waver in the sound. The speed of the waver is controlled by moving the LFO slider from "S," or slow, to "F," or fast. To get a "wah-wah" effect, follow the same procedure but set the Modulation switch to "VCF" instead of "VCO." If the CS-01 needs to be tuned to another instrument, the electronic pitch can be adjusted a little higher or lower with the "Pitch" slider in the VCO section. Moving the slider above 0 toward the "+" position gradually tunes all pitches higher. Moving the slider below 0 tunes all pitches lower. Normally the pitch slider should be left at 0.

The CS-01 is a monophonic, or lead, synthesizer. Like a melody instrument, it can be played only one key at a time. But through the many synthesizer controls, the sound can imitate almost any instrument, real or imagined.

One of the possible synthesizer panel settings, called a patch, is illustrated in Diagram B. These settings will generate a sound like that of a piano on the CS-01. Notice that the piano setting uses a sharp attack and

DIAGRAM B

Panel settings on the CS-01 for a synthesized piano sound.

DIAGRAM C

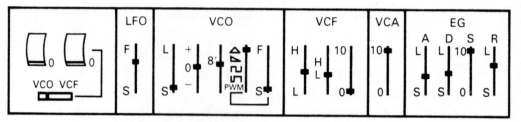

Panel settings on the CS-01 for a synthesized flute sound.

low sustain in the EG section. Diagram C shows panel settings to produce the sound of a flute. Note that the flute setting uses a softer attack and high sustain in the EG section. Adjust the LFO speed slider carefully to around mid-position so that the vibrato pulse sounds neither too slow nor too fast.

You can alter the flute setting to create a very good sound for trumpet, oboe, or bowed strings. First, switch the Wave slider to sawtooth wave. Move the Attack slider down to "S" for sharp attack. Then vary the Frequency Cutoff slider until the sound is exactly what you want. To further modify the sound to bowed strings, creating a string chorus effect, set the modulation wheel to 0. Switch the Wave slider to "PWM," or "Pulse Width Modulation." Then adjust the slider labeled "PWM Speed" to achieve a pleasant pulse in the tone. This regularly modulates the width of the rectangular wave-form so that the sound will have the illusion of a chorus of strings playing together.

With practice you can become sensitive to the small variations in slider settings that will give you the new sounds you like best. It helps to make a diagram of a particular panel setting, or patch, that you can refer to until you have it memorized. Larger synthesizers will have many more controls, but all of them will be based on the same sections incorporated into the CS-01: LFO, VCO, VCF, VCA, and EG.

Boss KM-60 Mixer • This compact stereo mixer handles up to six channels of sound. Each channel has individ-

A Boss KM-60 Mixer with six individual input channels and controls for volume, tone, reverberation, special extra effects, and stereo "panning."

ual controls for volume, treble frequencies, bass frequencies, special effects, and a control for determining how much sound is mixed to either the right or left stereo outputs.

The KM-60 may be mounted on a rack or used on any flat surface. First, set all volume knobs counterclockwise to the minimum level. Plug the power cord into a wall socket. Then check out the identical controls available for the individual channels. These are arranged in six vertical columns at the left of the facing panel and numbered from 1 to 6.

Start with Channel 1. The top switch is marked "ATT," or Attenuator. It has three positions to provide three different input levels for that channel. This switch must be set to accept a full signal, but not an overload, from the particular instrument plugged into the matching channel input on the top, or back, of the mixer. Use the loudest setting that still sounds clear. The control just below is a "Treble" knob for boost or cut of high frequencies. Place the knob at the center, "0," for normal flat response. Just below the treble control is the "Bass" control for low frequency boost or cut. Also center that control at 0 for flat response.

The next knob is marked "Effects." This controls any special-effects device with one cord plugged at "Output" and the other plugged at input for Channel 1 at the back of the mixer. With the control knob all the way counterclockwise there is no effect. As the knob is rotated, the Effects unit will begin to alter the sound on that channel. Below the Effects knob is the one marked "Panpot." This is a volume control which effects the output stereo channels. If the knob is set to left of center, more sound will come out of the left channel speaker. If it is set to right of center, more sound will come from the right channel speaker. And when the knob is centered the sound is equally divided between the two speakers. Below the pan control is the volume level knob for Channel 1. Channels 2 through 6 have all of the same controls.

To the right on the mixer panel are the controls for overall sound balance of the two output channels. In the center is the "On-Off" power switch. Just to the left is another two-way switch labeled "LCF," for "Low-cut Filter." In the "On" position it reduces the bass frequencies allowed to pass through the mixer, also reducing certain room noises, microphone noises, and rumbles.

The remaining knobs control volume for the two master output channels, which handle the blended signals from the individual inputs. At the top on the right are two VU, or "Volume Unit," meters with swinging needles. These show the volume level being handled by each master channel. Incoming sound causes a needle to swing to the right toward the 0 point. This means the input is at optimum level and can be handled well by the mixer. If the needle is driven further to the right, the sound will begin to overload the mixer and cause distortion. The master control for that channel, at the base of the mixer beneath the meter, should be set just low enough so that the loudest signals do not bump the needle into the distortion area and against the pin at the right of the VU meter. Above the master volume knobs are dials to control the volume of special effects present in each master channel.

As well as providing a check of the incoming volume level the KM-60 also accepts a headphone jack for sound monitoring. The headphones will give an accurate sense of the final sound being patched from the mixer to an external amplifier and speaker system. The blended tone colors, volume levels, and left-to-right stereo images of the various instruments all will be heard, and immediate adjustments can be made either with the master controls or the individual controls for each of the six channels. Volume for the headphone is controlled with the "Monitor Vol" knob.

Any number of channels from one to six can be used. When all six are used the mixer is very flexible. For instance, suppose a combo consists of a vocalist and five instruments. There then would be separate mixing inputs for voice mike, guitar, electric piano, combo organ, electric bass, and still another electric instrument or percussion. And up to six different special-effects devices can be added, one for each mixer channel. Thus reverberation, "wah-wah," fuzz box, phaser, chorus, and any other unit all can be handled by the KM-60. The effects can be controlled either at the mixer or by using each unit's own volume knobs, foot pedals, or foot switches.

For situations requiring more mixing channels, two KM-60 units can be connected and stacked vertically by means of stacking jacks provided on the rear panel, forming a twelve-channel mixer.

Each of the instruments described in this section can be comfortably handled by the Boss KM-60 Mixer, together with almost any stereo amplifier and speaker setup. And up to six processing devices can be added as well.

Many other choices and combinations of instruments and special-effects units are possible. Some of those currently available are pictured in the photographs in this book. And manufacturers are continually revising their equipment and offering new models and systems. You will have to learn through experience, but these suggestions and operating pointers can help you to begin selecting and using your own equipment.

FUTURE TRENDS IN ELECTRONIC INSTRUMENTS AND MUSIC

Current trends in the use of electronic musical instruments already are clear and can be expected to continue. The first of these is simplification: fewer or more efficient parts and overall design. Electronic technology is advancing on many fronts: space research; military defense; radio, TV, and satellite communication; computer science; energy research; and many more. An advance in any branch of electronic technology quickly becomes employed in other areas. And all such developments affect the design and manufacture of electronic music equipment. For instance, if a computer company makes a simpler circuit, if a space communication lab devises a better radar oscillator, or if a high-fidelity manufacturer develops a more efficient microphone, each of these advances may also bring improvements in the manufacture and performance of electric and electronic musical instruments. The instruments will perform better and will be more reliable.

At the same time equipment constantly becomes more sophisticated. More and more functions can be packaged into a unit without an increase in size. Even now an entire FM radio circuit can be manufactured on a chip the size of a thumbtack. Oscillators and other circuits all are becoming almost unbelievably miniaturized. This production sophistication enables electronic instruments not only to become smaller and lighter, and therefore more portable, but also to become more diverse. An electric piano that produced one kind of tone ten years ago may easily be designed to produce seven different tones today, and may be almost infinitely versatile ten years from now. Yet it

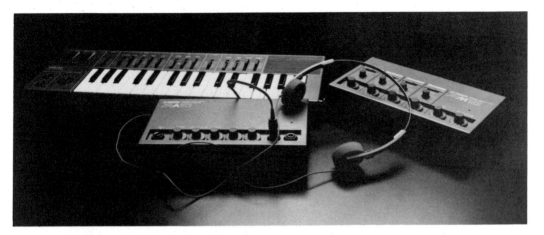

Electronic musical components are becoming smaller. The CS-01 synthesizer, stereo mixer, stereo headphone amplifier, and open-air stereo headphones pictured here—all part of the Yamaha Producer Series—are compact, battery-powered components.

probably will be no more complicated to operate.

One criticism of electronic instruments is that their sounds never seem to duplicate exactly those of acoustic instruments. This always has been partly true. A commercially produced synthesizer may use only one wave-form for all of the high and low pitches of an electronic trumpet sound, for example, while in reality the wave-form of a real trumpet sound will change somewhat according to what pitch is played, who is playing the instrument, how loudly or softly it is played, or how each tone fits into the flow of a particular piece of music. This simply means, then, that more elements of change, or *parameters*, must be included in the synthesized sound. Already, custom-designed studio equipment can control many increased parameters to achieve a more natural synthesized sound. And as technology improves and manufacturers compete for better and better sound, these improvements gradually will appear even in low-cost instruments. Thus, synthesized sound will continue to become more accurate, more flexible, and more "lifelike." Eventually, any performer will be able to produce as many subtleties of expression on electronic equipment as a musician using an acoustic instrument. There is no reason to assume that acoustic instruments ever will be totally replaced by electronic ones. But electronic instruments will continue to become increasingly popular as designs improve.

Another trend in electronic music is in originality of sound. Probably the best use of electronic instruments is not to imitate acoustic music but to explore facets of sound production and combination that never have been used before, achieving otherworldly results that will become commonplace in the future. This requires educating both performers and listeners to the new possibilities. Such education will follow several paths. Students in elementary schools and secondary schools will receive more sophisticated training in all sciences, including computer science, acoustics, and electronics. At the same time there will be more teachers who are well trained in the use of electronic instruments, both in school labs and private teaching. Thus more young people will not only use and listen to electronic music-making equipment, but will understand it better and play a role in developing the instruments and sounds of the future.

The use of electronic music in professional recording is also increasing. As electronic sound becomes less expensive and easier to produce and handle, it naturally will become even more a part of the common recorded sounds all around us. Disks and tapes played at home and on the radio, as well as sound tracks for theaters, films, TV, videodiscs, and other sight-and-sound combinations, will further merge purely electronic sound with electronic pictures and optical projection.

And of course there will be future discoveries and inventions scarcely imagined today, like entirely new ways of storing sound and building sound libraries. We may develop a totally controlled sound environment, eliminating all unwanted noises and tailoring all sound to suit the listener. Or perhaps there will even be equipment to convey sound impressions directly to the brain so that one can "tune in" internally rather than externally, thus changing even the basic definition of the word "sound."

Whatever the course for the future, it seems certain that electric and electronic instruments, with creative performers, composers, recording artists, engineers, and their new music and changing technology, are here to stay.

GLOSSARY

acoustic—using physical sound

amplitude—volume or quantity

audio—within the range of human hearing, from about 20–20,000 Hz

chord—two or more pitches sounded simultaneously

computer—electronic system for storing and processing encoded information

current—measured flow of electric charge

digital—using digits, or *binary numbers* (combinations of 1 and 0), to encode information

electronic—dealing with the properties of atomic electrons

116

envelope—time contour of a sound from its start to its finish, consisting of attack, decay, sustain, and release

filter—device for blocking selected frequencies

frequency—number of timed vibrations per second

fundamental—lowest frequency component of a musical tone

harmonic—following the musical overtone series in multiples of whole numbers

Hertz—cycles per second, abbreviated *Hz* (after Heinrich Hertz)

octave—interval of eight scale tones between notes of the same letter name; a two-to-one frequency ratio

oscillator—device for generating alternating current

oscilloscope—device for displaying an electrical wave-form

overtone—tonal frequency that is a multiple of the fundamental; also called *partial*

pitch—a musical note recognized by its fundamental tonal frequency

resonance—"sounding again"; sympathetic reinforcement of a vibration

reverberation—sound sustained by reflection or repetition

semitone—one half-step ($\frac{1}{12}$) of the musical octave

scale—ladder of pitches between notes of the same name

signal—information-carrying impulse of an electrical system

synthesizer—device for generating and manipulating electronic signals that can be amplified and converted to sound

timbre—quality given to a specific sound by the number and proportions of its overtones

transducer—device for converting one form of energy to another, for example, mechanical vibrations to electrical energy

voltage—force initiating the flow of electric charge

wave-form—shape, contour, of a single vibratory cycle as seen on an oscilloscope

white noise—random mixture of all frequencies in the audio range, resulting in no identifiable frequency

INDEX

References to illustrations are in **boldface.**

119